I WAS AN ABOMINATION

A Story of Trans Survival in Conservative America

SHERYL WEIKAL

TEHOM
CENTER

Tehom Center Publishing is a 501(c)3 nonprofit publishing feminist and queer authors, with a commitment to elevate BIPOC writers. Its face and voice is Rev. Dr. Angela Yarber.

Paperback ISBN: 978-1-966655-25-1

Ebook ISBN: 978-1-966655-26-8

CONTENTS

To every trans kid who just wants to grow up;
for every trans kid who never got the chance.

The trouble is that we have a bad habit, encouraged by pedants and sophisticates, of considering happiness as something rather stupid. Only pain is intellectual, only evil interesting. This is the treason of the artist: a refusal to admit the banality of evil and the terrible boredom of pain. If you can't lick 'em, join 'em. If it hurts, repeat it. But to praise despair is to condemn delight, to embrace violence is to lose hold of everything else.

— URSULA K. LEGUIN, *THE ONES WHO WALK AWAY FROM OMELAS*

INTRODUCTION

This is probably the first and only time you'll read a memoir where the author is beginning with a lengthy explanation of why she *didn't* want to write this book. There are a few reasons for that. The first is as simple as it is, frankly, lazy: Writing a book is hard, and after writing one already, I wasn't sure I wanted to do it again, particularly one which involved the emotional labor of recounting the most painful periods of my life.

The writer Blue Telusma defines "trauma porn" as "any type of media – be it written, photographed or filmed – which exploits traumatic moments of adversity to generate buzz, notoriety or social media attention."[i] There are times where that seems like the only type of literature or media trans people receive. Media is replete with stories of trans people being killed, committing suicide, being attacked. Even legal arguments about our rights before the Supreme Court, as with *United States v. Skirmetti*, devolve into arguments about our suicidality. Trans people are not our trauma, are not our pain, and yet to the cis (not transgender) world, there seems to be nothing *but*. Trans joy is rarely depicted, and trans love is similarly absent. On the other hand, trans pain, trans trauma, trans grief are ubiquitous to the point that those things are all we ever are. I frankly did not want to add yet more fuel to that fire. I am not my trauma. No trans person is their trauma.

Then there is the reality that I am, at best, a terrible messenger for this story, even if it is my own. Any trans person with even a modicum of a platform receives messages requesting that they write a memoir, and I am no exception. Yet I am, at the same time, a nobody. I'm a lawyer, yes. I'm the first openly transgender lawyer to argue at the Seventh Circuit Court of Appeals; I brought the lawsuit which codified the right of trans people to practice law in Illinois without being deadnamed, misgendered, subjected to genital inspections, or otherwise discriminated against. I wrote briefly about baseball for *Fangraphs* and *Beyond the Box Score*. But in the grand scheme of things, I am, at bottom, a nobody. I'm not famous. I'm certainly not rich, not after a career spent in consumer rights and legal aid. I definitely never intended to become a trans activist, even if that is a role I now hold, albeit reluctantly. And even if by some stretch someone *considered* me any of those things, I believed – and still do – that the last thing the world needed was yet another story by a white, cis-passing trans woman. In the trans world, racialized trans people and trans men are ignored, forgotten, subject to the twin discriminations of transphobia *and* racism, with the latter often coming as much from their white trans siblings as from the cis world. Then there are non-binary, agender, genderqueer, and other people who do not fit into the gender binary at all; their transitions and identities are no less valid than mine. Their stories and lives need to be centered.

And finally, quite frankly, the only time I wrote anything in detail about my story and upbringing – a piece for *Fangraphs* in 2018 – my parents threatened legal action. I honestly did not want to fight my family, even if they are fifteen years estranged, to prove that what I remember *did happen*, even if they don't want to admit it.

Those are all, or so I thought, very good reasons for not writing the memoir you now hold in your hands. And yet here you are, and here it is, so clearly something changed. My misgivings remain, particularly insofar as the book you now hold will almost assuredly fit some definition of "trauma porn."

And yet, with the re-election of Donald Trump to the presidency in 2024 on the strength of hundreds of millions of dollars of attack ads against my community, I felt, in all candor, that this story was necessary. For years, I have heard the denials of the existence of trans children from all corners of the political spectrum, Republicans and Democrats alike, but it's reached a fever pitch in 2024.

My favorite song lyric, by the musical artist Jewel from her anthem "Hands," is that where there's a man who has no voice, there ours shall go singing. My voice may not be the one that needs most to be heard at this moment, but I do *have* a voice, and when there are people in need it behooves me to use it.

I was a transgender child who grew up to be a transgender adult. I was not influenced by my school, because I did not go to public school after Kindergarten. I was not forced into it by liberal parents, because my parents were ardent social conservatives who believed any form of queerness was, in their words, an "abomination." (It is from that constant reminder that this book received its name.) And yet at eight years old, with complete conviction, I announced to my parents that I was a girl. It took me another twenty years to complete the journey, with a great deal of pain and trauma and heartbreak along the way, but the reality is that I always *was* a girl, despite years of efforts by my parents to deny and suppress that fact. I am writing this book, in short, to prove that people like me exist, in the vain hope that perhaps you, my reader, will stop denying reality when faced with the evidence of your eyes.

The increasingly popular idea, circulated by powerful billionaires like author J.K. Rowling and investor Elon Musk, that children cannot become transgender without the influence of an adult, is nothing but a transphobic myth. I know, because I was a transgender child whose parents – and every other adult influence in my life — overtly tried to *stop* me from being transgender. For so many of us, we are, as the popular song goes, born this way. Certainly many will dismiss my story, dismiss *me*, in order to suit their agenda. I do not pretend to believe that everyone will be persuaded that trans kids are as normal as anyone else. But if telling my story persuades even one previously apathetic or uncertain cis person that we are real, we exist, and that our identities are immutable components of ourselves, this book will have served its purpose.

But even that, by itself, wouldn't have justified telling this story. Rather, as Rebecca Nagle so brilliantly said in her book *By the Fire We Carry*, "the story lived in my body and I needed it to come out."[ii] I want today's trans kids, facing the weight of bigotry beyond reckoning, to know it really, truly, does and can get better. I know that seems a cliché, especially now, with our rights rolled back across the country. I know it seems bleak. I know if you're a trans kid yourself, you are probably reading this thinking that I have no idea what it's like to be a trans kid now, so how can I say it gets better? And you're right. I don't know what it's like to be a trans kid today. But I do know what it's like to be a trans kid. I know what it's like to grow up to be a trans adult, who gets married, who has a life and a career and a family and happiness. Yes, it's a fight to get there. No, it is not easy. No, you don't have to follow the same path I did; there are dozens of paths, and they're all valid. But I promise you, I am not special. Anything I can do, so can you – and you'll probably do it better.

So with that, I have a few notes. First, a content warning: This book features graphic details of sexual violence, suicidality, suicide attempts, self-harm, and child abuse. Please take care of yourself when you read this book, and only read it if you won't harm yourself in the process. Second, a few notes on language. I use "racialized" to refer collectively to people of the global majority, rather than the more white-focused "people of color." I use "cis," short for "cisgender," to refer to people who are not transgender, and "trans" to refer to people who are. Finally, consistent with the Jewish tradition of not writing out the name of the divine, I use G-d, with a dash instead of an o, to refer to the Jewish Supreme Being.

There are many events in this book, things I did, that I am not proud of. I could call them mistakes, but that would minimize them. It would be easy, and maybe even correct, to say that some of the things I did were under duress or without full knowledge of the harm they caused. But that would also be to deny my own agency and to shirk my own responsibility. For each and every one of them, and for all of them together, I apologize. An apology does not undo the harm, but it is owed nonetheless. I have included them in this book both because an honest retelling of the story of my life requires they be told, but also because this is not a self-aggrandizing hagiography. I am the sum total of my experiences and actions, for better and for worse.

What follows is my story, beginning with the formative years of my life, as best as I can recall it. For most of my childhood, I had no real notes to fall back on, and I have not spoken with my parents in fifteen years, but the memories are in most cases still fresh and vivid even now. That said, memory is fallible – years of law practice have taught me that – so please understand that although I have reconstructed the details with as much clarity as I can, errors are bound to be present. With luck, they will be minor. I cannot remember the exact details of conversations from 25 or more years ago, so what I present here is to the best of my recollection. I have also changed or omitted the names of many of the people involved to protect their identities.

Thank you for reading.

THE BEGINNING

Is the child to be considered as an individuality, or as an object to be moulded according to the whims and fancies of those about it? This seems to me to be the most important question to be answered by parents and educators. And whether the child is to grow from within, whether all that craves expression will be permitted to come forth toward the light of day; or whether it is to be kneaded like dough through external forces, depends upon the proper answer to this vital question.

— EMMA GOLDMAN

ONE

Like many immigrants, my paternal grandfather, Mote Klatzko, arrived in the United States through New York City from Lithuania. He was just nine years old when he and his parents reached New York in 1912, and just five years later, military records show he was on a transport to Europe to fight in the Great War.

My grandfather said that his name was changed involuntarily by immigration officials when he arrived, but I learned later – in researching this book, in fact – that wasn't true. In reality, some time between his return from the Great War and the start of the Great Depression, Mote Klatzko changed his own name to "Maurice Clarke," likely in response to widespread antisemitism. When in 1930 he became a naturalized United States citizen, the federal government listed his race on his application as "Hebrew" – a jarring reminder of how otherized Jews were in the early part of the last century.

Maurice had wanted to be a doctor, but a combination of anti-immigrant sentiment, antisemitism, and lack of money had conspired to sabotage those plans. Instead, he graduated pharmacy school from Fordham University, the only Jew in his class, and opened a store in Scarsdale, New York. This was at a time when pharmacists crafted and compounded the medications they dispensed, and my grandfather developed a reputation for serving anyone who came in, regardless of whether or not they could pay for the medicine they needed. My grandfather had the same reputation with the ice cream floats his pharmacy also served. As an adult, I would learn of my grandfather's connections with the Jewish socialist traditions of New York.

My grandfather met and married another Tobie Schachner, the daughter of Austrian Jewish immigrants who had also made their way to the New York suburbs. Tobie was twenty years Maurice's junior, but utterly devoted to her husband. They had one child: my father. Tobie's brother, Harry, had married Edith, a holocaust survivor. Edith never discussed what happened to her during the Shoah, but was one of the only members of her family to survive the camps, and never discussed what she'd experienced with anyone besides Harry; when, late in life, she lost her memory due to advancing dementia, Harry let slip to me that he thought that was, in truth, a blessing.

My father, during my childhood, often told me about how he grew up and came of age at my grandparents' pharmacy, donning a cape and pretending to be Superman for hours on end as his parents worked in the shop. He also told of a scary incident which happened one day when my grandmother accidentally spilled a hot baking mixture, severely burning my father and leaving scars across his chest and back; my father told me this so traumatized my grandmother that she never again thought of having another child.

Of my mother's family, I know little. My mother never let me or my sisters meet or speak with them, often telling me during my childhood that her father was physically abusive. She also told me her grandfather was Sol Engelhard, the founder of Sweetheart Paper Company, who had passed away before I was born, and for whom my parents named me. I do know that my mother's mother was the daughter of Jewish immigrants from Austria and Russia, but I know precious little about her father besides his service in the American military in World War II. When I reached out to my mother's family years later, I received a polite but terse and firm message indicating they did not wish to have any future contact. I respected their decision and left it at that.

My father grew up to be five foot eight, muscular, sporting the mustache typical of the 1970s and 1980s, which strongly resembled the bristles of a broom. He'd later shave that broom around the time I was born. He wore his medium-length black hair combed back simply. My mother, fifteen years younger than my father, was five foot six, slim, with piercing green eyes, brown hair, and unusually beautiful. "Call me DJ," she wrote in her high school yearbook, owing to the first two initials of her name: Donna Jo. She had been a child actor and model in commercials and television pilots through her teenage years, but even as a small child, I would note the stares and compliments she received about her appearance from men and women alike, from questions about her beauty regimen to asking if she was a model. Men following her, catcalling her – in grocery stores, in libraries, on sidewalks — was a daily event.

My father, the only child and son of Jewish immigrants, was a well-known disc jockey in Syracuse, New York. Much older than my mother, my father's combination of local celebrity and distinctive radio voice had made him sought after both in the broadcasting world and as dating material.

My mother told anyone who would listen how she and my father met. At nine years old and with a crush on the already famous disc jockey, she had marched over to him and said "I'm going to marry you someday." In my father's telling, he responded "that's nice," and did not see her again until they reconnected years later, when my mother was sixteen. In my mother's telling, they remained in constant contact through her teenage years until they started dating in earnest. The details are, frankly, disturbing either way, given the age difference between my parents and the implications of both versions of the story. In any event, my parents got married in April of 1986, and I was born two years later, the first of three children.

My father's parents, the only grandparents I ever knew, were staunchly opposed to the union between my father and mother. My grandmother, in particular, was suspicious of my mother from the start, and viewed my mother as marrying my father for his money rather than for love. My grandfather shared her concerns, but was more worried about losing a relationship with his only child, and future grandchildren, by taking a stand he knew was a losing fight.

My father wasn't a disc jockey by the time I was born, but only because he had moved onto more prestigious pursuits. My father spent the latter half of the 1970s and the first half of the 1980s as part of the White House press pool, covering Presidents Gerald Ford, Jimmy Carter, and Ronald Reagan. Of the three, my father was proudest of covering Reagan, whom he considered to be a personal idol. The basement of the house where I grew up was filled with awards my father had won from his on-air career and his time as a member of the press pool – and pictures of him with Reagan. My father loved regaling everyone who would listen with tales of how excellent a president Reagan was, and he particularly admired Reagan's lack of action regarding AIDS in the 1980s. My father also believed that Reagan was singularly responsible for the downfall of the Soviet Union and would tell me over and over again growing up that Reagan had saved the world.

Shortly before I was born just prior to the 1988 presidential election, my father was in a catastrophic car accident that broke his hip and spine and left him with a permanent speech impediment. Two surgeries later, including taking a piece of his hip to reinforce his spine, he was out of life-threatening danger, but doctors nonetheless told him that he would never walk again, to say nothing of resuming his on-air career. My father, however, proved them wrong at least in part by walking again six months later without completing his prescribed physical therapy. Part of that was his sheer determination, but part of it was also financial – with no health insurance, two surgeries to pay for, and a baby on the way, he needed to return to work. Moreover, my mother, who had rather enjoyed the financial benefits of being married to a formerly well-off and famous radio personality, had no interest in getting a job of her own. Thus my father went from being a radio personality to an audio engineer at the NBC television station in Washington, D.C., WRC-TV. It was a job he would have in some form or other for the rest of my childhood, and in many ways I very much grew up around that station. Every year my father would bring the whole family to the station with him on Thanksgiving, and sometimes on Christmas too, but sometimes he would just bring me, and I relished those times.

I don't remember the tiny apartment on the border between the District of Columbia and Silver Spring, Maryland that was ostensibly my first home, but I have fond and vivid memories of the little ranch-style brick house on Greer Avenue in Silver Spring fifteen minutes away that was my parents' starter home. They moved in shortly after I was born. There was a stained glass chandelier above the breakfast nook in the kitchen, a rocking bench on the side of the house, and a swing set in the compact backyard. It was, in many ways, a perfect picture of life in upper-middle class suburban America. There was everything but the requisite white picket fence.

And so, when I was of age, I started pre-kindergarten and then kindergarten at Montgomery Knolls Elementary School down the street on State Route 953. I didn't know it at the time, but those would be the only years I would spend in public school – or any other nonreligious school, for that matter.

I loved my time in Kindergarten, though it was not without its bumps. I could read before I could talk, and so when I walked into school for the first day of kindergarten, I said "Hello Ms. Scholnik" to the teacher and offered her my hand, having read her nametag. The teacher, who did not believe me that I had read her nametag, sent me to the principal's office for lying, whereupon the principal attempted to prove my deception by having me read from an encyclopedia in his office. I did so happily, not at all understanding that the intent of the exercise had been to prove that I could *not* read, and so I did not at all understand the astonished look on the principal's face after, having completed the assigned page, I flipped over and continued to the next. After all, no one had told me to stop.

I had been able to read long before I started school, a talent for which my mother credited herself. Perhaps that was true, but the reality was somewhat more complicated than that. Even at that age, I had a feeling that something was terribly *wrong*, something I could not quite put my finger on. It most presented itself with the simple fact that I did not recognize my own reflection in the mirror, a reality that would persist until I finally medically transitioned two decades later. I did not yet have the words to describe that feeling, of course, but even in kindergarten I *knew* I was supposed to be a girl, but I did not understand exactly why.

Reading, to my young mind, was a way to figure out what, exactly, was the source of this feeling. At first, I read everything with words on it, meaning that for years I read out loud every road sign on every highway, in case they might reveal some important information or secrets about the universe. This both greatly annoyed my father and led to some hilarious moments, as before I understood abbreviations I asked my mother what a "Delmembr" was. "Del Mem Br" was how the signs on I-95 abbreviated the Delaware Memorial Bridge.

Shortly after I was putting words together, I discovered to my delight my father's 23-volume Grolier International Encyclopedia; it seemed to four year old me that the sum of human knowledge was contained within its pages, and I read the entire tome over and over again. It was one of the first books I ever read. I did not learn what being trans was – there was, alas, no entry for that – but I did fall in love with dinosaurs, and began devouring every book on dinosaurs I could find. Thus, when Ms. Scholnik was reading us a book about dinosaurs one day in Kindergarten, I raised my hand and politely but firmly informed her that the book was incorrect, and "Brontosaurus" was not a separate species but in fact another name for "Apatosaurus," the earlier name for the same animal. I was correct, but found myself in that familiar chair in the principal's office, anyway. Undeterred, I wrote a letter to the publisher of the book, requesting they correct the error. In response, they sent me a pop-up book about dinosaurs. I was so proud of that book that I took it everywhere with me for months. And when I was cast as the ankylosaurus in the school play, I was thrilled.

Seventeen and a half months after I was born, my sister Sabrina arrived. My parents had intended to nickname her "Brina," but I could not pronounce that. Instead, I said "Biba," and the nickname stuck.

Sabrina cried a lot as a baby, and I found her crying fascinating. Not understanding *why* she was crying, and more out of sheer curiosity and interest than anything else, I would run back and forth from my mother to my father to Sabrina's crib, telling each of them "Biba's crying. Biba's still crying." When my mother got her a rocking chair to sit it, I rocked back and forth next to Sabrina's chair, helpfully telling everyone "Biba's still crying" as I did so.

At home, at school, I was never much good at keeping to myself. I had two friends: Jonah, a little white boy who sat next to me, and Danay, a little Black girl who lived across the street. Danay used to give me her barrettes to put in my hair, and she was also my very first crush; I loved her eyes and her smile. I even loved that when we would swing together on the swing set in the backyard she would always manage to reach higher than me. Jonah confused his c's and k's, so I would try to be helpful by fixing it for him in his writing book, and then get sent to the principal's office each time. I frequented the principal's office in those days, but never quite understood it was for disciplinary purposes, so to me the principal was just my friend who I stopped by to visit. My parents, however, were less amused, and after a semester of this, had me transferred to a different class.

The new teacher, Ms. Bullman, was older and sterner, with short gray hair and a serious disposition. Rather than send me to the principal's office, she just never called on me, and in the end, bored with learning letters I already knew and sounding out words I could already read, I just sat in the corner and built dinosaurs out of Legos. I had no friends in the class, and missed Jonah, Danay, and the principal terribly. (I still had not realized the principal was not my friend.) But I still got to see Danay after school on the swings.

My parents, inveterate lifelong racists, did not approve of Danay. My father, who listened to Rush Limbaugh and Sean Hannity religiously during my childhood, believed that slavery had been beneficial to Black people because it had kept them from committing crimes, and would often opine on what he saw as the unfairness and anti-white racism of affirmative action. (Anti-white racism was a myth, of course, and there was nothing good about enslaving people at all.) Thus, when Danay's family moved in across the street, they had been as mortified to see a Black family as I had been thrilled to see a girl my age. My parents forbade me from speaking with her, an edict that I, with my typical respect for authority at that age, entirely ignored. I understood neither my parents' racism nor their instruction; as far as I was concerned, she was my friend and I loved her, so that was that.

One day in school, a white girl began harassing Danay and throwing rocks at her. Danay came to me and asked me for help. It was a racist attack, but I did not understand that; all I knew was my friend was being mistreated, so I concluded that throwing rocks back at her attacker seemed appropriate, and did just that. Two rocks hit their target, her attacker began bleeding from her head, and this time instead of the principal's office I was just sent home with a note for my parents. Ms. Bullman had instructed me to not read the note, so of course I read it anyway, prompting even *more* recrimination when I began reciting its contents at the subsequent meeting between the principal and my parents.

An appropriate reaction may have been for my parents to explain that although it was good to protect my friend, I could have done so by notifying an adult or confronting her attacker with words instead of resorting directly to violence. My parents did not have that reaction.

After the incident with the rocks, my mother had me tested for autism. She never told me the results. I found the entire experience unpleasant and ended it by arguing with the test taker because the certificate she gave me at the end was grammatically incorrect, which did not in any way endear myself to the staff there. My mother later said it was this test taker who recommended I be homeschooled, but I have no idea if that is really true. All I knew was that after a year of kindergarten, my parents pulled me out of Montgomery Knolls. I never got to say goodbye to Jonah or Danay. That was the end of my formal grade school education.

Meanwhile, having told my mother I found her treatment of Danay unacceptable, I had – at four years old – resolved to run away. I did not know or understand what racism was, but I knew unfairness when I saw it, and so with my usual level of bravado, I packed a single pair of underwear and my teddy bear into a bag, informed my parents of my plans, and off I went. They didn't try to stop me.

"Bye bye!" I waved cheerfully to my parents as I walked out the door, bag slung over my shoulder.

"Bye bye!" they waved back, fully knowing what was about to happen.

I made it all the way down the street before I became hungry, realizing that I had selected my dinner time for my great escape. Food was of great importance to me in those days; earlier that year, I had actually gotten my parents kicked out of an all-you-can-eat pizza buffet that advertised kids as eating free after I had eaten more than a few entire large pizzas myself. And so around I turned back to the house for dinner, prematurely ending my excursion.

A year later, we left Silver Spring for good. As racist as ever, convinced that Danay's criminality was rubbing off on me from all of our time together, they decided to move us as far away as my father's job would permit. Sabrina was just three when my parents decided to move the family out of Silver Spring, so she had no memories of the house we were leaving – but I did. And when I finally understood that we were moving, I was devastated, not wanting to leave Danay. As my parents packed boxes, I would take every item I could lift out of the box and put it back where it went. When my parents asked me why, I expressed my desire to stay near Danay, and that revelation brought my participation in the packing process to a swift and decisive end.

My mother, in particular, was insistent there be no Black people around in our new neighborhood – an instruction made all the more perplexing by the fact that they hired a Black realtor, Mr. Isaac, to sell the house on Greer Avenue.

It was after his first visit that my parents mentioned race for the first time. They asked me if I had any questions after meeting the realtor (which I had done with great zeal, because I liked meeting people and had no idea we were moving). I responded in a rather uninterested tone that I did not, and began rolling my little Ernie and Bert *Sesame Street* truck around the kitchen. My parents insisted on discussing the matter, much to my chagrin. They told me that, like Danay, he was Black, and asked if I had any questions about Black people. I thought for a moment (mostly about how I would rather be playing with my Ernie and Bert truck), looked at my mother, and asked, completely seriously, "What's Black?" My mother told me that his skin was darker than ours, and I, having legitimately never noticed this before, asked again, still completely seriously, "Is that important?"

That was the first time I ever saw my mother angry. It would not be close to the last.

TWO

To find them a new house, my parents hired Mr. Bosher, a real estate agent with a brand-new Dodge Grand Caravan that we'd all pile into to be shown houses. In an effort to meet my father's requirement of no more than a one-hour commute to WRC, he drove 80 or 90 miles per hour down I-270, which did not amuse my mother in the slightest. After being shown several homes in western Maryland and southern Pennsylvania, my parents selected a two-story house on a farmette in a town called Mount Airy.

Mount Airy is part of rural western Maryland. If you start on I-70 in Baltimore and continue due west, the city gives way to trees as you enter the Baltimore suburbs and, after a while, farmland. There's a reputation of Maryland as an urbanized state, but away from the metro areas of Washington DC and Baltimore, rural farmscapes spread over rolling hills as you approach the Catoctin Mountains, a branch of the Appalachians that divide the East Coast from the rest of the continent. Mount Airy is the highest point between the Catoctin Mountains and the Atlantic Ocean and was, at the time we moved there, almost entirely rural. The town was so small, in fact, that when my mother informed my father's parents of the pending move, my grandmother, unable to find the place on a map, asked if there was running water there.

She was not far off. Mount Airy was at the time a two-stop-light town, but both were yellow flashers rather than full traffic signals. The only anchor store in town sold animal feed from a single outdoor strip mall that also housed the post office and, oddly enough, a karate studio. We lived off of Watersville Road, which intersected with West Watersville Road on one end and, confusingly, Watersville Road West at the other. I say "off" of Watersville Road because although Watersville Road was (mostly) paved, Newman Drive, the road on which our house sat, was a mix of gravel and dirt under the best conditions. The views were breathtaking – a farmette surrounded by farms – but it was remote, with a well and septic instead of city water and sewer because Mount Airy *had* no water and sewer.

My parents were so desperate to get out of Silver Spring that they closed on their new house in Mount Airy without ever ensuring it would be move in ready when the time came, and even agreed to a leaseback provision for the sellers. Thus, we moved out of the house in Silver Spring only to find the Mount Airy house still very much occupied, and suddenly we had nowhere to go. In retrospect, it's the sort of comeuppance you'd hope for people who move across the state based solely on racism, but at the time, this led to a family of five – my sister Elaina, five years younger than me, was born just before we moved – living in a hotel room in a Comfort Suites in Glen Burnie, Maryland.

The hotel was expensive, but my mother resented it greatly. Only a few years before, my father had been a famous, wealthy DJ with a glamorous, if small, apartment in a desirable building; now, five of us were living in a single hotel room with two queen beds. Now that my mother was "homeschooling" us, she insisted that my father get as many jobs as possible to pay for it. As a result, by the time our stay in the hotel ended, my father was working three jobs, usually in the same day: the night shift

(4 pm to midnight) at WRC, the graveyard morning shift at Black Entertainment Television ("BET"), also as an audio engineer, and as an adjunct professor teaching late morning classes in audio and broadcasting at Towson State University. My father was rarely, if ever, in the hotel room as a result.

The hotel stay wasn't just a few weeks. It was so long, in fact, that the Olive Garden restaurant, which had not yet broken ground our first day at the Comfort Suites, was open to customers before we left; we even ate there once before our time at the hotel concluded.

For me, the hotel was a strange time. The feelings of wrongness were intensifying, but I still couldn't put words to them. Being away from Danay and Jonah left me terribly depressed, and I began to lose the intransigent, defiant stubbornness that had defined me to that point in my life. What made matters worse was that my mother's "curriculum" consisted of me sitting and watching an Olive Garden restaurant being built next to the hotel. My mother thought this would be "life experience," but I found it unbelievably boring. Sometimes my mother would drive us up to the hill overlooking our future home and we'd just sit there, watching. This was a weekly affair until Sabrina asked my mother during one such excursion, "Are we homeless?" My mother cried herself to sleep last night, and we didn't return to the hilltop after that until after we'd moved in.

One weekend, my mother decided to visit the house where the sellers of our new home had said they were moving, only to find they'd moved in weeks before and were using the farmette as storage. Embarrassed, they agreed to vacate the property, and we moved into the home where I'd grow up.

7240 NEWMAN DRIVE was a two-story house with a finished basement, with a long paved driveway at the very end of the dirt and gravel washboard road. Newman Drive featured a steep grade, so you couldn't really see the house until you were almost at the top of the hill, and with the house being at the end of the road, there was nothing but open fields in three directions. The house sat on a few acres of land, a long, narrow plot with a large backyard and larger front yard. At the time, though it had been sold as a farmette, the house was the only building on the plot.

Best of all, for my parents, it was an enclave in which they could be sure they'd have total control over how they raised their children. Though both were observant Jews who insisted on attending services at shul weekly, keeping kosher (Jewish dietary laws), and putting mezuzahs on every door, they felt that keeping their children away from "bad influences" – Black people, and later gay people – was most important. My father had introduced my mother to the nationally syndicated right wing talk radio shows of Rush Limbaugh, Sean Hannity, and Mark Levin, and played all three in our blue 1992 Dodge Caravan whenever we went anywhere. From them my mother learned about Dr. Laura Schlessinger, the 1990s right wing provocateur who framed her homophobia and racism as a family advice call-in show; my mother insisted we listen to her show every morning, from beginning to end if possible. They received their news from the "Paul Harvey News and Comments" which broadcast at noon every weekday, after Schlessinger's show was completed. It would not be hyperbole to say that my parents listened to six or more hours of conservative talk radio daily, and attempted to have us listen to as much as possible as well.

My mother's devotion to Schlessinger was so complete that she had the three of us complete a fundraiser for Schlessinger's nonprofit foundation every year in hopes of getting mentioned on the show. There weren't any stores or homes around in Mount Airy, of course, so my mother would drive us to Frederick, to Damascus, to Baltimore, to go from door to door, asking store managers to donate school supplies and money. Then we'd listen to see if we would be mentioned on the show. The year we succeeded, my mother taped the show and played it over and over again.

From Schlessinger, my mother received a deep paranoia that any contact at all with public schooled children would turn the three of us – myself, Sabrina, and Elaina – gay. Schlessinger preached "family values" of cisheteronormativity, abstinence, sex for procreation only, and antipathy for LGBTQ+ people, abortion, and contraception. My mother, insistent that she would not be the mother of a gay person and with a fervent belief – derived, of course, from Schlessinger — that being gay was a choice, began daily lessons which explained that being gay was an abomination to both G-d and nature, with special attention to me. As my parents' firstborn child and ostensibly their only son, my mother was particularly insistent that I "carry on the family name." Daily lectures on the importance of family continuity – that I marry a "nice Jewish girl" and "have Jewish children" – took place in the car, at grocery stores, even at shul. My mother told me there were two things she considered mortal sins, for which she would sit shiva for me – that is, consider me to be dead to her – being gay, and marrying someone of another race.

My mother's homophobia was so all-encompassing that it very nearly caused the only ever schism in my parents' marriage. One day, when I was about eight, I told my mother excitedly about the televisions I'd seen at my father's office and the movie previews and programs playing on them. One of them had shown a couple of boys my age hugging each other. My mother decided this was gay, and read my father the riot act to the point where she actually kicked him out of the house; the next two nights, he slept at the television station. Eventually they reconciled after he persuaded my mother I had invented the entire story because he would never expose her children to anything containing queer people. I was harshly punished for a lie that was true, because it was easier for my father to say I was lying than to confront my mother about her homophobia.

At first, despite the isolation, living on the farm did nothing to dampen my headstrong nature. Shortly after we moved in, my parents showed me the animated film *Pocahontas*. Having read the entry for Pocahontas in Grolier Encyclopedia a few years earlier, I was dismayed at how little the story portrayed on screen resembled her actual life story, and even more upset at how the character of John Smith had been made heroic. I carefully watched the credits to find out who the producers were of the movie and then wrote them and Disney a letter asking them to apologize to Indigenous people for making such an inaccurate movie. They never responded, which prompted me to write a second letter, and then a third; my mother refused to mail any more.

My grandfather, of blessed memory, never lived to see the house on Newman Drive. It was not without a valiant struggle. My grandfather had inflammatory bowel disease at a time when modern biologic treatments didn't yet exist. Even after the colitis turned into cancer, my grandfather continued to fight, dismissing warnings from his doctors that he would not live to see the birth of his grandchildren. He held all three of us before he passed, and, remarkably, did so on his own terms. When the end was coming, he stubbornly refused to eat the bland, soft, fiberless diet required of patients with inflammatory bowel disease, opting instead for his favorite meal: pastrami sandwiches, on rye bread, with a pickle. It was about the worst thing a person with the condition could possibly eat, and my grandmother let him know it, in a conversation that would play out over and over again.

"Maurice!" she would exclaim. "You cannot eat this! Let me make you something else."

"Tobie," he responded. "I'm dying. You think a sandwich will kill me any faster?"

And then he would happily eat his sandwich.

From my grandfather I would inherit his inveterate stubbornness, his left-wing politics, his large feet, and his Crohn's

Disease. Given the virtues of the first two, the latter two seemed a small price to pay.

After my grandfather's death, my grandmother was alone in Scarsdale in a house she could ill afford to take care of. Elderly, lonely, and in declining health, my grandmother wanted nothing more than to either move in with her son or to have us move closer to her.

My mother, however, would not hear of it.

It was not for lack of room or financial ability. Even after the tens of thousands of dollars in medical bills my father had accrued to pay for his surgeries and treatments after the car accident, my parents were still comfortably upper middle class. A four bedroom, two story house on significant acreage is expensive, even if it was in the proverbial middle of nowhere. Instead, my mother increasingly feared outside influence on how she'd raise her children, and my grandmother – who, like her husband, was unabashedly politically progressive – threatened that. My father, of course, was politically conservative, but he and his parents had simply decided not to discuss politics so as to preserve their relationship. My mother had no such compunctions, leading to arguments I would personally witness each time we would make the six-hour drive north to Scarsdale to visit my grandmother. One time, for instance, my grandmother objected to the homophobic, anti-abortion rhetoric of Schlessinger, and said as much. Instead, she recommended that my mother try listening to Dr. Joy Browne, who hosted a radio advice program for 20 years and was, unlike Schlessinger, actually a psychologist. My mother refused, and openly accused my grandmother of attempting to corrupt her children. Browne, it seems, was insufficiently homophobic.

One day, when I was seven or so, unable to sleep, I walked downstairs and found my mother watching some late-night talk show which had the late fitness instructor Richard Simmons leading a routine. She was cursing the television as she watched, mumbling as she often did about "Sodom and Gomorrah" and the degradation of society. I went over to her and, as young children often do, informed her of my insomniac plight. My mother, however, had more important work. Seizing my shoulders, she pointed me in the direction of the television.

"That's Richard Simmons," she began.

"Oh," I said, utterly uninterested.

"He's a gay. Do you know what that means?"

"Yes," I said. In fact, I had no idea what it meant and just wanted the conversation to be over, having suddenly decided I could figure out how to sleep after all.

"It means he has a lot of sex with the same sex," she said sternly. I had no idea what any of that meant, or why this was so important, and my sudden yawning revealed that this was all very uninteresting to me. My yawning, however, only urged my mother on. "Do you know how disgusting that is?"

"Oh so he has a lot of affairs?" I asked, trying to muster up the sincerity my mother seemed to want. The only thing I had learned from all of the hours of listening to Schlessinger was that affairs were bad, so I took my best seven year old guess despite not knowing what an affair was. I had figured I would know one when I saw one. I had figured incorrectly. My mother sighed, asked, "Why are you like this?" and sent me back to bed.

My mother's greatest fear from then on was that I would turn out to be gay. She had been terrified before, but now her fear became an obsession. Daily she would beseech me to remember how important it was that I grow up into a "red blooded American male" and remind me about Richard Simmons and how much I should *not* be like him. I still did not really understand what being gay really was, or why it was so terrible. And I definitely hadn't made the connection between being gay and the feelings of wrongness which were now becoming a crisis.

Around the same time, I was sitting in my parents' bedroom watching television. I was transfixed by the show, an episode of *Star Trek: The Next Generation*'s first season called "The Arsenal of Freedom." That episode became one of the most formative moments of my life. In it, an artificial intelligence created by a long-dead civilization of arms dealers attacks the crew of the Starship *Enterprise*, including a landing party that includes first officer William Riker, operations officer Data, and security chief Natasha Yar. From then on, I was a lifelong Trekkie, adoring everything about *Star Trek*. My father would joke that in the summers, I obsessed over the Yankees and baseball, and the rest of the year, I was obsessed with *Star Trek*. (He wasn't wrong.) But more importantly, watching Denise Crosby's Yar, I had an epiphany.

Oh, that's what I'm supposed to look like.

I didn't know what "transgender" was. I had never met any trans person, and wouldn't for years. I didn't know transitioning was possible, and wouldn't for years. But what I saw in Tasha Yar was a more accurate reflection of myself than what the mirror showed me, and *that* was what I understood.

A year earlier, spooked by the reflection in the mirror that seemed like it belonged to someone else, I had told my mother "my face is wrong." I didn't yet understand *why*, but I knew the reflection wasn't right. Everyone told me that what you saw in the mirror was your own face reflected back at you, but my brain insisted *that was not me in the mirror* and I told my mother as much.

"I like your face," she said simply, "and it's really hurtful to me that you would say otherwise."

I tried explaining further that my face was wrong because it was not *me*, but I didn't have the words to explain it and ended up grounded for my trouble.

But now, watching Crosby's Tasha Yar walk around the very 1980s set that served as the planet Minos, I had a flash of understanding. I had never wanted to grow up to be a man. But she was what I was supposed to grow up to be. I was supposed to look like *her*. Not her blonde hair or being in Starfleet, mind you. *Who she was.*

Now it would be easy for someone reading this to conclude

that I just wanted to imagine myself as Tasha Yar in the same fanciful way a child might imagine themselves as a horse or a starship captain or a baseball player. This was, to the contrary, not close to the same thing. The sense of girlhood I had was not something I chose, not something I developed from watching *Star Trek: The Next Generation*. Rather, all that episode did was give me the means to *recognize* my girlhood for what it was, as though someone had shone a spotlight on the part of myself that I had been struggling to identify. Being told I was a boy had been *wrong*, and now I understood why. Tasha Yar was simply the personification of how I already saw myself.

On some level, I understood that the bits between my legs had to go. They weren't supposed to be there. In my mind, this meant there had to be some easy-detach mechanism, like a toy which splits into two parts when you only want to play with one part of it. So I grabbed onto my testicles and pulled, hard, waiting for the click that would never come. When that didn't work, I took the zipper of my onesie pajamas and tried to use that for leverage, placing them in the open zipper and trying to use the zipper to tear through the skin. It never occurred to me this was harmful because *it wasn't supposed to be there.* Yet even as blood began seeping from the spot, the skin remained stubbornly in place, the testicles undamaged and unsevered.

This would be harder than I thought.

FROM BIRTH, my sister Sabrina was my parents' favorite child. Sabrina had inherited my mother's looks, with soft brown eyes in place of my mother's green, and with the musical talent my mother had always wished for herself. Sabrina was legitimately a musical prodigy, by the time she was five or six, she was excelling at piano lessons. Originally my mother had signed me up for piano in the vain hope that I would be the musical talent she so desperately wanted, but, as with most things in my childhood, I would prove to disappoint her. I enjoyed the instrument well enough, but had no real feel for the craft and even less desire to practice. I loathed sitting still, and was far happier building something – be it *Star Trek* ships with Legos in my room, or forts out of sticks in the endless fields around the house – than sitting on a piano bench for an hour or more at a time. Thus my mother ended my piano lessons and gave them to Sabrina instead.

I was heartbroken, but not because of the loss of the piano. Frankly, I didn't really care one way or the other about it. But my mother told me flatly how much of a disappointment I was, calling me lazy and spoiled and telling me I was a waste of her time and money. Desperate to please her, I begged her, crying, to let me try them again. My mother was unmoved, and my punishment for wasting the money on piano lessons and refusing was being told to sleep outside, on the deck, in the cold.

It was the first time my mother would punish me in that fashion. It would not be the last.

Sabrina and I had a complicated relationship for our entire childhood. Her strengths were my weaknesses. Brilliant, beautiful, artistic, even from a young age she was deliberate with her every decision and patient to a fault. By contrast, I was impulsive, always in motion, impatient. Sabrina was emotional and emotionally intelligent, able to evoke feeling through her music, through art. I was analytic, logical, mathematical. From an early age, I saw the world through a binary lens. Things were either fair or unfair, right or wrong, black or white. When Danay had told me about the rocks being thrown at her, I simply threw rocks back. When Jonah spelled something wrong, I fixed it. I saw no shades of gray, an irony if there ever was one for a child who was – and remains as an adult – profoundly colorblind. And so in those years I was unafraid to tell my parents when I thought they were wrong, including writing detailed letters explaining the flaws in their logic. Sabrina, on the other hand, embodied nuance. I, quite frankly, envied her: her grace, her creativity.

My mother fostered between us an enmity and naked competition that would last through our college years. Through this point in my short life, my personality had been punctuated by headstrong impulsiveness, insatiable curiosity, and a sheer refusal to take no for an answer about anything. Being out of school had made these tendencies even more pronounced; when, to fulfill the state of Maryland's requirement of science credits, my mother invited over an astronomer to teach us a lesson about how orbits work, I peppered him with questions. Sabrina sat quietly and obediently and took notes, whilst I asked question after question, trying to understand everything, challenging the astronomer to explain every concept. My mother prided herself on proving that homeschooled children were better behaved than our public schooled counterparts, and thus found my behavior deeply embarrassing – and that was the last time I was ever allowed a guest teacher besides my mother. Another time, whilst the three of us were at the grocery store with my mother, another woman remarked on how polite we were.

"You have them well programmed," the woman said.

"Well, except this one," my mother responded, patting my head.

In addition to everything else, Sabrina grew more quickly than I did, too, meaning that until my thirteenth birthday she was taller than I was, sometimes by quite a bit. This was fine by my mother, who was more than happy telling people that the quiet, artistic, well behaved Sabrina and I were twins – or simply that Sabrina, and not I, was the oldest child. My mother would often remind me at seven or eight that I was "a juvenile delinquent" for my actions with the rocks, or that I had very nearly been arrested.

"If I'm not hard on you, you'll end up in jail," she'd say. "Is that what you want?"

Still, to this point the threats didn't have much effect on me.

Oh, I understood them, and I was fully aware that Sabrina was my parents' favored child, but I saw no reason to change anything about myself. Moreover, my mother's incessant demands that I behave better were interspersed with demands that I literally could not comply with. For example, it became very clear early on that I was profoundly colorblind, unable to distinguish red from green, blue from purple, orange from pink or red, green from brown, and so on. Still, my mother was convinced that she could teach me to see colors anyway, and would publicly chastise me for getting colors wrong, whilst bragging that she'd taught a colorblind person to see colors on the rare occasion I would get lucky on a wild guess.

As for Elaina, she was so much younger than either myself or Sabrina that at this point in our lives, she was just the baby of the family, sucking her two middle fingers happily on car rides and asking for every balloon in sight. Unable to pronounce "balloon," she'd simply say "ballallallallalla" over and over again until someone gave her one, then hold it happily, grinning from ear to ear. With her other hand, she'd hold mine in a peculiar way, insisting on holding only my pointer finger as tightly as she could. I loved her with all my heart.

Then one day Elaina got an ear infection.

My parents distrusted doctors. My father, a vaccine skeptic, believed that homeopathic so-called remedies were more effective than conventional medicine. Colds he treated with an elderberry cocktail called Sambucol. Bacterial infections he treated with garlic pills instead of antibiotics. Each morning after breakfast and each night he wasn't working, we'd all line up in the kitchen for the array of pills and herbal concoctions he'd insist we take as prophylactics, cold treatments, or just for general health. Elaina couldn't swallow pills yet, so he'd mix hers into applesauce.

It turns out, however, that garlic pills and homeopathy aren't an effective cure for an ear infection, and Elaina's right eye began to swell. My mother *finally* at this point took her to a doctor, who prescribed her an antibiotic for what was now cellulitis. My mother didn't bother giving her the antibiotic, however, opting instead for more garlic. Nevertheless, when the next day Elaina's eye was twice its normal size and Elaina asked why there were "two mommies," my mother blamed the doctor for not being more aggressive with her treatment.

What had been an ear infection, and then a sinus infection, and then cellulitis, was now a periorbital abscess – that is, a pocket of infection literally pushing Elaina's eye out of its socket. The next day, when Elaina's eye was the size of a baseball and swollen shut, my parents finally took her to the emergency room. The tiny local county hospital realized this was beyond their purview, and she was transferred by ambulance to the nearest Children's Hospital, where she spent the next week.

Whilst Elaina was in the hospital, my father took Sabrina and me to the station with him during his work shifts. Despite my worry for Elaina, I was having a grand time, especially when my father took us to different places for dinner. One day, he took us to a food court, and whilst standing in line for slices of pizza, handed me a ten dollar bill and asked me to get lemonades for everyone from the kiosk next door. I looked around, saw the kiosk, but then realized there was a kiosk across the court with less expensive lemonades. Thinking my father would be proud of me, I ran over, got the lemonades, and came back with more change than my father expected.

My father was furious. What I hadn't understood was that my father had selected that lemonade not for the price, but because it was, well, real lemonade, and what I had purchased was a lemonade-flavored drink with no actual lemon juice in it. To punish me, my father had me drink all three lemonades in place of my dinner.

"Mmmmm, chemicals," he said with each sip.

Elaina's attending physician at Children's Hospital was Dr. Jafar, a kindly Muslim doctor with a friendly, compassionate demeanor. He wanted to surgically remove the abscess. He hoped he could save her eye, but knew he could save her life. My mother, however, did not trust the "Arab doctor" and demanded second and third opinions. A young white resident provided the answer she wanted: Wait and see, and decide against the surgery. The resident believed that risking the eye of a three year old was unwarranted. Yet with each passing hour, Dr. Jafar noted the infection growing closer and closer to Elaina's brain.

This led to an out and out argument between my parents. Sabrina, at 7, knew enough to stay out of it. I, at 8, did not, and completely unsolicited, provided my opinion that they should do what the doctors recommended. It was entirely in character for me – headstrong, consequences be damned, rushing in where angels fear to tread – but my parents had had enough. After an hour of the two of them taking turns excoriating me for my audacity, my mother quietly told me that she wished it were me lying in the hospital bed instead of Elaina. Maybe then, she said, I would learn some humility.

Later that day, my parents opted for the surgery. Dr. Jafar saved Elaina's life. He saved her eye too. There wasn't even a scar.

THREE

S abrina loved horses since before she could talk, and my parents wanted to oblige her. It was typical of my parents' approach to her. When she began piano lessons, my parents – at no small expense – had an antique piano moved from my grandparents' house in New York to the farm in Mount Airy, then painstakingly restored. Each week, it seemed, she'd have new pairs of shoes, with shoeboxes stacked high in her bedroom. Horses, though, would take a bit more doing than shoe shopping.

Though the land where we lived was a farm, it was one in name only when we moved in. There was only a house and empty land. A couple of zoning changes and a court date before a judge changed that, and my parents brought home an appaloosa named Bucky. Bucky required a barn, and pastures, and so I spent weeks helping my father build. We dug holes for fence posts with a manual post hole digger, placed pressure treated 4 x 4s in each hole, and strung tension wire between the posts. Of course, my father had never farmed before; he was an audio engineer from New York with no farming experience, after all. Thus, it wasn't long before the posts started to bend over, and we realized we'd made a terrible mistake: We hadn't put any cement in the holes before inserting the fence posts. Further, since the holes were only a few inches deep, the posts blew over in the wind – to say nothing about the pressure placed on them by a fourteen hand, thousand-pound horse. Thus, only weeks after the fence was finished, my father and I were back in the field with a backhoe, pulling the old posts out and drilling new ones with an earth auger.

My parents, already receiving earfuls from my grandmother about our move to the middle of nowhere, knew my grandmother would be unamused by the addition of a horse. To that end, they forbade us from mentioning Bucky, the barn, or the new fences to my grandmother during our weekly phone conversations. I thought this unfair, of course, and mentioned it anyway, not understanding at all the logic behind keeping from my own grandmother an issue of what seemed to me to be such self-evident importance as the acquisition of a horse. My mother, exasperated, eventually told me that the fence and horse were supposed to be a surprise for my grandmother, which I briefly accepted before asking how they could be a surprise for my grandmother if they were intended for Sabrina.

After the mishap with the fence, my father did his research when it came to building a barn. I helped my father lay a proper foundation from concrete, frame walls from treated two by fours, and attach shingles to plastic-flashed plywood and particle board for the roof. The barn began with just a single horse stall and room for hay, straw, and bedding, but it wouldn't stay that way; it expanded seemingly every year with more stalls, more storage, and more rooms as my mother collected more and more animals. Within five years, we'd have two horses, a dozen chickens, fifteen cats, five dogs, two dozen gerbils, guinea pigs, iguanas, hamsters, dozens of fish, turtles, rabbits. There were over a hundred animals at the farm, which now consisted of the house, the barn, two chicken coops, and various other side buildings my father would build with my help.

My mother called it an animal rescue, but really, she was just collecting animals. Some were legitimate rescues – as in, we adopted them from real animal rescues, like two enormous Great Danes named Rocky and Duchess, or a little Yorkshire Terrier named Tucker (whom I nicknamed Schmeegle for his penchant to wheeze and pant in a manner more than a little reminiscent of the creature Smeagol from *the Lord of the Rings*). Rocky was so big that his long tail knocked over cans on the kitchen counter; he was six foot four inches on his hind legs and over 250 pounds in his prime, yet he was so sweet natured that I could ride him like a horse when I was little.

Some were born there – my mother was gifted two barn cats, let them reproduce, and before long we had fifteen cats in a giant cat run. Two of the rabbits were presents for Sabrina from my parents. Some, my mother embellished or outright lied; she rolled over a box turtle with her lawnmower, then claimed the cuts all over the box turtle – which had miraculously survived – were from a sinister experiment by public high schoolers with razor blades. She also claimed a small horse they'd purchased was actually a rescue because she believed that because the sellers were gay, they must have sodomized the horse with a baseball bat. And when the care for the animals became expensive – horses and fields required a tractor, and all those animals required feed and bedding – my parents created a nonprofit they called "Heaven's Gift Animal Rescue," though it was less an animal rescue and more my mother collecting animals. Then my mother planted an orchard of fruit trees, and fields of pumpkins and squash.

My father may not have known much about farming – at least at first – but years as an audio engineer were proof positive of his prowess with mechanical and electrical systems. He had a keen mind for machines and circuits alike, able to visualize systems in his mind and then build them. Whenever he was home, he was probably working on some project or other, whether it was building the electrical systems for the barns and other outbuildings – in which he installed lighting, heating, and fans – or laying water lines to bring drinking water to not only the barns, but the chicken coops, the orchards, and the fields where the horses grazed as well. We had two cars – the bright blue 1992 Dodge Caravan that was the ubiquitous family hauler of that era belonged to my mother. My father drove a Pontiac 6000 station wagon from the 1980s with over 300,000 miles and a sagging headliner that by my tenth birthday leaked a quart of oil per day. My father insisted on trying to keep the wagon alive, and very nearly succeeded; each weekend before work, he would jack up the car and try his latest idea to solve the oil leaks. He'd lay under the wagon and tinker, and I would stand next to the car and hand him whatever tools or materials he asked for. His attempts were so successful that the much newer Caravan went through two transmissions before my father finally had to trade in the wagon.

In fact, what spelled doom for the wagon turned out to not be a mechanical failure at all. Station wagons make poor farm trucks, and the rapidly growing menagerie needed hay, and straw, and feed in large quantities – not to mention the need to visit veterinarians and farriers. The Caravan, which seemed to blow another transmission when sneezed on, was obviously not suitable for labor of that kind. And the wagon simply didn't have the power or torque necessary for pulling a horse trailer, despite my father's efforts to beef up the wagon's suspension and transmission. Plus neither car really was suitable for hauling the massive quantities of compost and manure produced by what was by this point a population of hundreds of animals. Thus, my father bade farewell to the wagon and brought home a two-door 1994 Ford F-150, with an extended cab so the whole family could ride in it (at least, in theory) and an eight foot bed. The truck had a lift kit, too, which made it particularly imposing to me at the time.

I loved that truck. It was the first car I ever drove. It started when my father – always, of course, when my mother wasn't around – let me take the wheel whilst sitting on his lap when driving it around the horse fields. Later, when I was tall enough to reach the pedals, he'd sit next to me as I drove it to and from the compost heap, or to and from the barn, filled with hay. And of course, he'd ask for my help when wrenching on it, for it replaced the wagon as his weekly project. Humorously to me, my mother, who hated the truck, never figured out that the truck was an F-150, instead referring to it by its trim level as "the XLT."

The remote and rural nature of the farm also meant that it was frequented by hunters, who would every weekend march down the easement between the fields into the woods on the far side of the house. After a few hours, shots would ring out, and the hunters would shortly thereafter return the way they came, one of them inevitably with a large buck slung over their shoulders. The first time I saw this, I sobbed for hours about the fate of the poor animal, and was concerned that if the trend continued, the deer in the nearby woods would soon be wiped out. After a time, I learned that the number of deer hunted was tightly controlled by the state, but my concern for the fate of the deer morphed into a concern for animals whose lives were not so protected, and for the first time I learned about endangered species.

I genuinely did not understand how people could fail to protect animals to such a degree that they went extinct, and I became determined to do something about it. At seven, I wrote to the governor of Maryland, Parris Glendenning, and asked him to do more to protect endangered species so none would go extinct. He (or rather his office) wrote me back promising to protect endangered species in Maryland (though he did sign the letter), and I hung his letter in my bedroom proudly. But I wasn't satisfied with his answer because I had just read that there were so many endangered species *not* in Maryland, so a few weeks later I wrote to President Clinton, asking him to save all the endangered species everywhere in the world. Clinton's office sent me back a postcard thanking me for writing him, and I hung that in my bedroom too.

BY THIS TIME, the truth of my inner girlhood had reached a crisis point. After my epiphany watching *Star Trek: The Next Generation* a year earlier, I had tried multiple times and multiple ways to remove the offending bits from between my legs, all unsuccessfully. Every night I dreamt of an illuminated platform in a forest, shrouded by leaves and branches and covered in glitter, onto which I could step and shed my skin, revealing my true self – my *girl* self – underneath. That I was going to need my parents' help to solve this was becoming more and more evident, yet after the negative reaction I had received from telling my mother my face was wrong, I anticipated a similarly negative reaction here.

Even at this point, however, I had never heard the word "transgender." It had never occurred to me that I was gay, either: Like most eight-year-olds, I had no romantic or sexual desires for anyone, and despite my mother's daily lectures about the abomination of homosexuality, I had made no connection whatsoever between that and what I assumed was just a fixable mistake in my body. I did not recognize myself in the mirror because the mirror showed "boy" when it was supposed to show "girl." I did not recognize my name because my name implied "boy" when it was supposed to imply "girl." I felt disconnected from my body because my body was assigned male when it was supposed to be assigned female. That was what I understood. I lacked this kind of sophisticated vocabulary to describe it, but I understood the feelings well enough.

My first attempts to come out to my mother were clumsy: I went over to my mother and told her I wanted to pretend to be Kate Mulgrew's Kathryn Janeway instead of Robert Duncan McNeill's Tom Paris the next time I was, whilst playing, pretending to be someone from *Star Trek*. I even began reciting

Janeway's lines from an episode of *Star Trek: Voyager* I had seen that weak, doing my best to mimic Mulgrew's distinctive voice.

"Look!" I said. "I can sound just like Kathryn Janeway. Maybe I can look like her, too?"

I wasn't quite prepared for what happened next. My mother grabbed my arms, knelt in front of me, and with an anger mixed with desperation she growled at me in a low voice, "Don't let me ever catch you doing that again. Do you hear me? Never. Again."

To be fair, coming out implies that I *knew* I was coming out, or that I knew I needed to come out. In truth, neither is accurate; I simply knew I needed help to swap out the boy parts for girl parts since I was unable to do so on my own, and did not recognize, let alone understand, the cultural taboos I would be breaking merely by asking the question. All I knew was my parents would be upset, though I did not know why. Besides, given how often I made them upset, it seemed to me an inevitability anyway. Besides, maybe my mother had simply not understood what I was getting at. I genuinely thought, at worst, she was insulted that I did not sufficiently appreciate the body I had, not understanding there truly was something wrong with it.

A few weeks later, my parents took the three of us to a build-a-bear workshop store in a mall for a get-together of home-schooled students. This kind of event was required by the state to show that homeschooled kids were receiving sufficient socialization, but in truth, I'd never met any of the kids there before, and we all just sort of kept to ourselves. But this was my opportunity, so I took it. Instead of building a bear, I built a stuffed doll of my true self, my girl self. She had short dark hair, like me. She had dark eyes, like me. She wore my clothes, or at least a reasonably accurate doll-sized facsimile of my clothes. But she was also unmistakably a girl, and so to drive the point home, I named her "Jane."

And then, right there in the workshop, I presented Jane to my parents, explaining that Jane was a Very Helpful Guide to show them what had gone wrong when I was being put together, telling them that she was what I was supposed to look like. Using Jane as a model, I asked, could they please help me to fix the problem?

And then all hell broke loose.

The car ride home consisted of my mother saying to my father, over and over again, at various levels of volume, "Coleman, your son made a doll of himself *as a girl*," and my father insisting she calm down because she could not possibly have properly understood. Upon reaching home, my parents dismissed my sisters to their rooms upstairs and, when they were sure my sisters could not hear us, asked me for clarification.

Still not understanding, in one final act of defiance, I once again repeated that Jane was me. I was Jane. I needed their help to fix myself.

"How many times have I told you that my son will not be a goddamn faggot?" my mother asked in a low voice. I searched those striking green eyes for compassion, for empathy, for understanding, and found none. I never would find any there again. My father urged my mother to calm down, to no avail. I carved the word "faggot" into my arm with a fingernail, so I could look it up later. I still did not know what was going on.

Thus began what would become an all too familiar tradition: My sisters dismissed upstairs either to bed or to play, I would sit at the kitchen table, listening to a lecture from my mother on the evils of queerness, waiting for the lecture inevitably to escalate to something else, something worse. I'd carve a word into my arm, usually one repeated over and over again by my parents, like "faggot" or "lazy" or "disappointment." When my father was home, he'd give the lecture. His lectures were worse. Pointing to the analog clock on the wall, he'd tick off the seconds.

"That second's gone. That second's gone. That second's gone. Those are seconds in your life you're never going to get back.

Your life is now shorter, and my life is now shorter, and it's because you won't man up and take responsibility. Do you know what it is to be a man?"

My coming out moment launched my mother from home-schooling into Christian conservative homeschooling. Shortly after I had made Jane, I found that my mother had chosen, for the first time, a structured curriculum for the three of us she'd obtained from Calvert School. My father built large bookshelves out of wood and converted what had been our living room into a school room. Later, she changed the curriculum to Bob Jones University and then to Veritas Press. She simply removed the references to Jesus from the various materials, but kept the rest, including references to creationism; I recall her telling my father that she'd rather deal with questions about Jesus than me being queer. My mother was even more obsessive about ensuring that we listen to Schlessinger's show now.

My mother became a teacher at the Hebrew School of the synagogue in Frederick where we were members and, in order to make sure that they were teaching "family values," she added to the lesson on the Ten Commandments an eleventh. "Man Shall Not Lie Down With Man," she wrote proudly on the blackboard for her students. (She also added to her students, all of whom were seven or eight years old, that Bill Clinton had violated the commandment against adultery, and insisted they tell their parents that Jews could not vote for him or any other Democrat lest they ratify his actions.) Meanwhile, I would spend hours at the synagogue library, fascinated by the books of Midrash and Talmud (Jewish legends and commentaries). One day, when I found the Talmud teachings on gender – which references eight genders – I noted the *"saris adam,"* someone assigned male at birth who becomes a woman instead. This was the closest I had ever come to a recognition of what I was, so I brought the passage home to my mother.

What had been daily lectures about the evils of being gay now took a darker turn.

"You are your father's only son," my mother hissed. "It is your sacred obligation to carry on the family name. And now you want to throw it away – for what? For your own selfishness? Your arrogance? You are positively the most arrogant child I have ever seen. Your father deserved so much better than *you*. You should be ashamed."

For the first couple of years, my parents' first attempts to de-trans me were mostly verbal. I'd be dragged out of my room for long lectures at the kitchen table, in the basement laundry room, at the barn whilst mucking stalls. Their goal was to persuade me that being gay was an unforgivable sin, that it was an abomination, and that if I chose to be gay, I'd be an abomination too. They insisted being gay was a choice, that I could simply choose not to act on any gay impulses, and that I owed that to my father. But I was still confused. I hadn't had any talks or lessons on the facts of life with them, and I didn't at all understand what, if anything, being gay had to do with the fact I was a girl. (As it turned out, I was indeed gay, or, more accurately, bisexual, but I didn't know that then.) Each time I would ask them, it would only make them angrier.

And then, one day, the hitting began.

The day's lecture began as many did, with the lecture. As per usual, my sisters were in their rooms or outside playing; I honestly don't remember which. I was only half listening, carving words I did not know into my arm with a fingernail to look up later, but also because the pain from letting out some of the blood distracted me from the existential pain of this incessantly wrong body. There was a certain morbid curiosity from carving words like "arrogant," "disappointment," "abomination" into your own flesh as they were flew from the mouths of your parents. In between words, I was counting the sheaves of wheat in the wallpaper pattern on the kitchen walls. I was ten years old or so, and only barely paying attention. Yes, yes, I am a terrible son. I know.

And then my father took his belt off.

"I promised I would never do this," my mother said. "But this is how my father disciplined me. Maybe this is the only thing you'll understand."

My father whipped the belt, and the leather end snapped into the table a foot away from me.

"Stop being gay and be a man," he instructed.

"I'm not gay," I protested, still having no real idea what being gay was or what it had to do with being a girl. The belt snapped again, this time making contact with the table eight inches away from me. I curled into my chair to make myself a smaller target.

"*Stop being gay and be a man*," he instructed, his voice sharper now.

"Why don't you believe me?" I asked, suddenly very much paying attention. The tears were coming now, not so much from fear as from sheer confusion. *I did not understand.* I was telling them what I was. Why was that bad? What had I done wrong?

The belt snapped again, contacting the table six inches from my exposed hand. I slid my hands under my buttocks. I was bawling now, begging my parents to stop. The confusion had given way to fear.

"**Stop being gay and be a man**," he bellowed. I looked to my mother.

"Mommy please I don't understand!"

My mother was unmoved. Her eyes were like emeralds – shining and beautiful, yet devoid of warmth. She shrugged.

"You brought this on yourself."

The belt snapped again. Three inches from my shoulder, the belt slammed into the table. I was resigned to the inevitable now, knew the pain was coming, knew there was nothing I could do, because I did not know what to say to stop it even if I wanted to.

"Is this what it will take to make you a man?" my mother asked.

The belt snapped again, and it didn't hit the table. I felt the pain in my shoulder, and again, and again. I closed my eyes and waited for it to end.

FOUR

Even today, there are few, if any, national guidelines for homeschooling. Defended by its powerful national lobby, the Homeschool Legal Defense Association ("HSLDA"), the industry – for, like most everything in the United States, homeschooling is, at bottom, a for-profit enterprise – is loosely regulated by a patchwork of laws that vary state by state and sometimes even county by county or city by city. Thus, even in otherwise progressive states there were few, if any, government checks on what homeschooling parents could or would be allowed to do.

Even in the 1990s, Maryland was developing a reputation as a reliably Democratic state, yet at the time that moniker was incredibly misleading. True, the last time Maryland voted for a Republican president was 1988, the year I was born, and by ten years later had twice voted for Bill Clinton by significant margins. Yet statewide races were far closer, owing to the state's divided demographics. The population centers of Baltimore County (home to Baltimore City), Montgomery and Howard County (affluent suburbs of Washington, D.C.)., and Prince George's County (less affluent DC suburbs) reliably voted Democratic. Yet outside the population centers, in the more rural areas of Carroll, Frederick, and Washington Counties in the central and western parts of the state, for example, voters were far more conservative. Democrat Parris Glendenning defeated Republican Ellen Sauerbrey in the state's gubernatorial race by a mere five thousand votes in 1994, with both my parents having voted for – and made calls – for Sauerbrey. When Sauerbrey – in a foreshadowing of what would a couple of decades later become a typical Republican play – refused to concede and accused Glendenning of voter fraud, my parents were firmly on board with her claims. When Sauerbrey accused Black people of voting multiple times and of Glendenning having procured the votes of dead people, my parents – like many rural Marylanders — believed her. For the rest of Glendenning's two terms as governor, my parents told everyone who would listen that he had stolen the 1994 election. In rural central and western Maryland, that was a view shared by most people they met.

Thus, Montgomery County – where Silver Spring was located, and where our house on Greer Avenue was – had stricter regulations on homeschooling owing to its more liberal politics. But our house in Mount Airy was located in more rural – and *far* more conservative — Carroll County, which at that time barely regulated homeschooling at all. Every six months, a social worker employed by the county would come to our house and speak with my mother for a couple of hours, ask to see us briefly to check we were present and alive, and then leave. My mother found even these biannual meetings a distasteful example of government overreach, complaining that she shouldn't have to show the government what she was teaching her own children. Thus, she often showed the county reviewer plans for lessons that didn't exist, or book reading lists she'd never assigned us. Thanks to the HSLDA, the reviewer wasn't allowed to speak with us, so there was no way to check.

Later on, the rules in Maryland changed, and beginning when I was about 14, the county review process required a biannual meeting at the County's Department of Education, where the county reviewer would be permitted five or ten minutes to interview a child being homeschooled. Of course parents were not just allowed, but *required* to be present during this interview, and of course that essentially made the entire process completely pointless as a check on potential abuse. Yet my mother found these interviews to be an example of "communism." My mother realized fairly early on that I was well spoken enough to handle these interviews, and so for a full week before each interview, we would practice constantly what I was to say. My job was to take up so much time that the reviewer didn't have the ability to ask anything of Sabrina and Elaina, and my photographic memory meant I could simply regurgitate anything asked of me by the reviewer to ensure I was doing reading, writing, and arithmetic at a grade-appropriate level. The interviewer would inevitably be too struck by my recitations of various literary passages to do anything else but sign off, like a passerby too distracted by a street magic show to notice the presence of a pickpocket.

It's entirely accurate to say that if homeschooling were actually regulated in Maryland – if we were subject to checks more often than every six months, or if I was interviewed outside of my parents' presence – my childhood would have played out very, very differently. It would be unfair and untrue to say that homeschooling is itself abusive, because I am sure there are a great many parents homeschooling their children who are loving, caring, and doing it for the right reasons.

My parents, on the other hand, were none of those things. It wasn't that my parents were unintelligent; my father had a master's degree from Syracuse University and later would earn a doctorate as well. My mother, too, was smart, but not educated, although she had flatly lied to me, to the county reviewers, to the state of Maryland, about her own educational background. To hear my mother tell it, she had wanted to be a lawyer, had been offered a seat at Seton Hall law school, and had been forced to drop out before attending after running out of money. In reality, it was her brother who had been accepted to law school, and he had actually attended and graduated. My mother had never applied to law school or attended a four-year college, instead receiving only an associate's degree. Degrees are hardly an indicator of intelligence, but her lie would have a profound impact on my life.

To my parents, homeschooling was a way for them and other similarly minded parents to protect their children from the influences of gay people and Black people, which they saw as more prevalent in public schools. My mother believed that I had been left abandoned in Ms. Bullman's class because she needed to spend more time with Black students, who my mother considered to be less intelligent and therefore requiring more time from the teacher. My parents were avid believers in the racist pseudo-science that formed the basis for Charles Murray's 1994 book *The Bell Curve*, and my mother often spoke of that tome as vindicating her own racist "theories." My parents were also vehemently anti-abortion, preaching that it was akin to murder and often taking us to anti-abortion protests and rallies. My mother also believed that a woman's place was as a homemaker, not with a career, and openly said career women should not be allowed to have children. My parents both believed it was a sin for a woman to work outside the home at all.

My parents weren't alone in these beliefs. In the United States, the homeschooling movement in the 1990s was led by evangelical Christian conservatives, and thus it was nearly impossible for my mother to find any likeminded home-schooling parents who weren't evangelicals or groups without an evangelical bent. At first, my mother made an effort to avoid them and simply crafted her own curriculum, reading us Jewish texts she'd find in the many Jewish bookstores around Baltimore. That meant frequent trips, and I loved to wander around the bookshelves, skimming volumes of the Midrash and Talmud and looking through the shelves of kippahs (traditional Jewish head coverings), mezuzahs (scroll boxes affixed to doorposts), and tallit (Jewish prayer shawls). This meant that the three of us learned Hebrew as well as English, a gift that grounded us in our Jewish identities. For secular learning, my mother read to us books like Kenneth Davis' *Don't Know Much About History*. And had our curriculum continued like that, it may have been unobjectionable – overt Zionism aside.

Yet, crafting a complete curriculum for three young children was no small task, and as we grew older it became harder and harder for my mother to keep up. Thus, by the time I was 8 or 9, my mother had all but abandoned her reticence to joining groups of homeschooling parents. The members of these groups made no effort to hide their racism and homophobia, and my mother would sometimes invite fellow homeschooling parents to our house for coffee and to inveigh upon the moral decline of the United States being presaged by the presence of Black people and "pushing the gay agenda" in public schools. They exchanged notes about public schools being "bastions of homosexuality" and "socialism," and my mother wasn't shy about sharing her beliefs that public schools were a socialist plot to lead to interracial marriage. In her mind, homeschooling was "saving" her children from the corruption of liberal values which she saw as inevitable in public schools. In this, my mother and her evangelical counterparts found common cause. They also found commonality in Zionism, with every single evangelical homeschooler being a strong supporter of Israel. Of course, to a person, this was because of their belief in the rapture, the evangelical end times myth which requires that Jews be in Israel to die en masse to bring about the resurrection of Jesus. My mother never much cared *why* these evangelical Christians supported Israel, instead assuring us they were examples of good allies to Jewish people. Despite this common ideology – or perhaps because of it – my mother would inevitably feel betrayed when some of her new friends would begin asking to see our family's horns, or use "Jew" as a verb, or attempt to convert us from Judaism to Christianity. Antisemitism as a theme in right wing politics was something my mother refused to accept as a problem, and thus was surprised over and over again when it happened.

Yet even as my mother cycled through evangelical friends who would come into and leave our lives on a regular basis, their influence lingered. My mother accepted their recommendations of curricula, and thus before long we were being taught not by my mother reading texts from the Jewish bookstores or the local library, but from books of the Calvert Christian curriculum that had a decidedly evangelical bent. My mother would at first have us skip pages which overtly mentioned Jesus, but in the end she gave up even that.

Instead, it was more important in my mother's mind to keep out the truly bad influences from the household. We were only allowed to listen to country music; all else, especially pop, rock, hip-hop, and rap, were banned. Classical music and oldies, music from the 1950s and 1960s, were only permitted with either my mother or father supervising. Anything we wanted to read, whether it be at a bookstore or the library, had to be first be read and approved by my parents. Television was explicitly off limits except for shows my parents had viewed and approved in advance – certain *Star Trek* episodes, the Christian drama *Seventh Heaven*, the Pax network shows *Doc* and *Sue Thomas, FBI*, and *Leave It To Beaver* were the only television allowed. The only exceptions were when my father persuaded my mother to let us watch a Yankees game, and even then we were ordered to turn away from the screen during commercials. Movies were similarly controlled, with Cecil B. DeMille's *The Ten Commandments* being the most frequent showing. Years before modern conservatives would use "woke" as a sort of slur to refer to queer people and people of color, my parents used "liberal" in much the same way. We were urged to avoid the "liberal bias" of the "mainstream media" and taught that if we watched mainstream news, we would be indoctrinated into being gay. As if to drive this point home, my mother hung a sign in the living room we used as a school room which read:

An Eye is Watching You
An Ear is Listening to You
And everything you do and say
Is Written Down in a Book

Portraits of Ronald Reagan also hung from the walls, along with *Hatikvah* (the Israeli national anthem). My mother also thought it important to have a curriculum that made us straight Zionists who married fellow white people. The Jewish grounding, she thought, would come from elsewhere. And so, we kept strictly kosher – with separate sets of dishes and silverware for milk, meat, and pareve dishes. We drove an hour to the kosher butcher in Baltimore, Wasserman and Lemberger, and the kosher grocery stores, Katz's and Shalom Kosher. We attended services every Shabbos at a conservative congregation in Frederick and later an ultra-orthodox one near Baltimore. I wore tzitzit (Jewish prayer fringes), had my own pair of tefillin.

Sabrina and I both attended Hebrew School at whatever synagogue we attended, but those programs were usually an hour each on Tuesday and Thursday nights, one season out of the year. My mother thought that sufficient to satisfy the state's requirement of socialization time, which was ironic because she forbade us from spending any additional time before or after class. These Jewish communities were politically progressive, focusing on the values of *Tikkun Olam* (repairing the world) and the universality of human rights, and that put them in direct conflict with the values of my parents. At first, this would prompt my mother to give long lectures on the way home from shul explaining why she thought the Rabbi was wrong. One time, when the Rabbi prayed for the so-called "two state solution" in the middle east, my mother called him a turncoat and said that G-d gave us all of Israel – including the West Bank, Gaza, and all of Jordan, Lebanon, and Syria — so it is not up to the Rabbi to question G-d's wisdom. Another time, when the

Rabbi said peace was the highest Jewish virtue, she told us that seeking peace was little more than weakness and people like the Rabbi had caused the Holocaust. When the Rabbi talked about the importance of civil rights, my mother's lecture on the way home was that Jews supporting the civil rights movement was a mistake because Martin Luther King, Jr. had been a terrorist who diluted what she called "Judeo-Christian values."

"The day we can afford it," my mother often said, "we are making Aliyah (moving to Israel)."

Yet that day never came. Living a few states away was one thing, but my father wasn't going to leave his mother, my grandmother, in another country entirely. My grandmother had no interest in emigrating; in fact, she privately told me one Shabbos morning she had grave concerns about Israel, and when Prime Minister Yizhak Rabin was assassinated, she saw the country as what her parents had been running *from* when they came to the United States. Then, by the time she passed away when I was 17, both Sabrina and I were in college.

The irony of my mother's Zionism was how Christian it was. Like many Jews, she supported a Jewish state. Yet the more time she spent around evangelical homeschoolers, the more her Zionism turned from Jewish self-determination into something more akin to Christian manifest destiny. This is not a metaphor; she often said in history "lessons" that G-d gave North America to white Europeans just as G-d gave Israel to us. Her belief in this kind of divine right and her racism and Islamophobia were a self-reinforcing feedback loop that continued for as long as I knew her. There were still donations to the Jewish National Fund and trees planted in Israel, but the Zionist protests she had us attend were not Jewish but explicitly Christian, featuring Christian country singers like Clint Black and Christian speakers like John Hagee. She voted for Bob Dole and George W. Bush twice; Clinton, she said, would have sold half of Israel to the Arabs. Bush, she said, knew how to "deal with them." When George W. Bush announced the invasion of Iraq, she was overjoyed, and openly told me she hoped the war would last long enough for me to have the opportunity to kill Arabs there.

She even found a website that played a song that went

"Time to bomb Saddam, blow him to Kingdom Come"

It was a sloppy, racist rhyme, but my mother found it deeply entertaining, and so she played it over and over again, then went around singing it to herself.

But her evangelization didn't stop her from using public schools as a threat. In fact, my mother would often threaten to send my sisters to public school if they acted out. I was different. My mother rarely threatened me with public school, instead threatening me with military school or forced enlistment. When at 13, I said I wanted to become a Rabbi when I grew up, my mother was in literal tears. To her, me becoming a Rabbi would be a betrayal of our family values, choosing the peace and tikkun olam of progressive Judaism over the militant Zionism my mother espoused. My mother's dream for me was that I would be a soldier, either for the American or Israeli military. If I eschewed military service, she thought I could at least be a politician. So great was her anger at my choice of profession that she told me flatly I would not be welcome in her home if I became a Rabbi. And so I apologized and dropped it. Yet she brought it up from time to time as a sign of what she saw as my weakness.

Maryland had physical education requirements for home-schooled children, which my mother only sporadically attempted to have us meet. At first, in years she didn't just falsify the records, she would have us do farm work for PE; split-ting large logs into cords of firewood with a sledgehammer and wedge or axe was a one of my mother's favorite things to assign to me. When the county reviewer objected, she signed Sabrina and me up for a homeschool group's intramural softball league, which was for me a dream come true. I saw myself starring on the field like Bernie Williams, the switch hitting Yankees outfielder whose swing I would painstakingly emulate with any stick I could find on the farm. As it turned out, I had none of his talent. I had no defensive ability to speak of at any position and was equally inept fielding grounders and catching fly balls. What I could do, albeit with no plate discipline, was hit. Despite a predilection for swinging at everything pitched to me – including offerings that bounced in or flew high and wide into the other batter's box – I had an uncanny ability to make contact and surprising power for my small frame. Occasionally I would hit a long fly ball that would draw oohs and aahs from the handful of parents watching, and I relished the attention, knocking imaginary mud off my shoes like a Yankees hitter might before digging in again. I wasn't any kind of natural hitter or anything – the quality of opposition was hardly challenging and I would have been overmatched in nearly any public school league with kids my age – but I loved it all the same.

It was because I loved it so much that after only a season, my mother ended our involvement in the softball league. I'd had a love affair with the Yankees ever since my father, himself a Yankees fan, had introduced me to baseball with the 1995 American League Division Series; the first at bat I ever saw was a single by Charlie Hayes. Before long, I would take any excuse to grab a bat or a stick and any tennis balls I could find and spent hours in the backyard or an empty field, throwing the ball up in the air and hitting it as hard as I could. I had no friends, so I would make up elaborate game stories to myself, announcing every at bat of fictional games to myself as I would toss the ball up, hit it, evaluate what the result might be if the ball was fielded by imaginary defenders. I would sneak out anyway, hit the ball anyway, for my imaginary team was the only company I would have.

My favorite times in those days were the rare occasions my father would pack a picnic lunch and bring the whole family to watch the airplanes land at what was then still called National Airport across the Potomac River from DC. There was a park called Gravelly Point, just across the river from the runway, that provided biking trails and grassy knolls with perfect views of the landing planes. The long drive and my mother's disdain for the mostly Black parkgoers meant that we rarely went, but I loved watching the MD-80s take off and land, and thrilled at the roar of the jet engines.

Video games weren't something my parents would allow, but my father had an old Atari 7800 console attached to an ancient cathode ray tube television in the basement, near his awards and many pictures of Reagan. Most Sunday mornings, my parents and sisters would sleep in, and I was responsible for watching the animals and keeping them quiet so they could do so. I had to wake up at 5:00 am, but I didn't mind, though, because I could sneak into the basement and play on the Atari without permission. The dogs would come with me and go to sleep, and I would play games like *Galaga*, *Ms. Pac-Man*, *Xenophobe*, *Super Huey*, and *Baseball*. Occasionally I'd get caught if my parents woke up earlier than expected, but it was worth it.

Though there was always plenty of work to do on the farm, I found I enjoyed gardening, and every year planted small plots of my own. The underground stream that fed our well was shallow near the side of the house, a perfect spot for a garden. I planted and grew potatoes, onions, tomatoes, and peppers, with great success. Other attempts – like pumpkins, cucumbers, and squash – were rarely as successful, usually for lack of room. Still, I loved gardening because it gave me time with the soil that wasn't for anyone but myself, and that would grow scarcer and scarcer as I grew older.

FIVE

"The center of calm" was the name I gave to the part of my spirit I assigned with keeping me sane during those years. Actually, "sane" might be the wrong word; as I got older, I was increasingly unsure of whether I truly was sane at all. I had no friends, I was isolated from everyone except my parents and sisters. "Grounded" might be a better word. I visualized it as a marble in the middle of my soul, surrounded by lightning and wind yet unaffected by the spinning maelstrom surrounding it. It was where I went in my mind in the early years of my parents' attempts to de-trans me, whether it was the belt or the lecture.

Our time at synagogues was more for my mother's edification than it was spiritual fulfillment, and that made it hard for me to maintain relationships even in Hebrew School. Once, at a bat mitzvah for a cousin about my age, my mother volunteered me as the entertainment for the after services reception. People asked me to recite the presidents backwards or name the vice presidents in order, spout facts about random countries, perform complex math problems in my head. I had no knowledge of this ahead of time, however, and was blindsided by suddenly being the center of attention. Still, I answered all of their questions, not understanding why they responded with applause, calling me a freak. The praise, of course, went to my mother, whilst I was a curiosity, a zoo animal on display. It was one of only a handful of times I ever met that cousin; my mother had no actual interest in relationships with extended family. Instead, this provided my mother with the opportunity for what she craved most: attention and praise. She was beaming ear to ear afterwards, whilst my entire body was shaking.

My mother thought it had been a big success, and began to book "performances" for me elsewhere too. The worst part was that after a time, I began to enjoy them – or at least, convince myself I did. That was, after all, the only positive attention I received, and the high from it felt addictive. But like a drug, it was unhealthy; the core of the thing wasn't that I was smart, but that I was a freak. And it gnawed at me even as I wanted more.

That, combined with the constant dreams of my girlhood contrasting with the onset of puberty, led my body to start to betray me. Shortly after the lectures started, I began having periodic episodes of diarrhea and nausea. At first, I thought it was simply from nerves, but it didn't take me long to realize that my anxiety was a *response* to the nausea, not its cause. I was nervous *because* I was throwing up; I wasn't throwing up because I was nervous. My parents didn't understand or didn't care. One time, my parents took us to a diner for dinner after a day at an amusement park where I rode a roller coaster for the first time. It was, for me at least, a rare excursion, and after ordering my food, I started to feel a familiar nausea. That led to a panic attack, and the panic attack made things worse, and I eventually threw up in the diner bathroom. My parents weren't concerned; it was impossible, they said, to be motion sick hours after a roller coaster. Instead, they were furious that I had ordered food I did not eat, and frankly accused me in front of my sisters of inventing my illness for attention. But the bouts became worse, and more frequent, and before long I was vomiting multiple times a week.

A doctor, of course, was out of the question. Months earlier, my parents had been insisting that my gait, in which my right foot pointed out to the side, was morally wrong, and they would physically force me to walk with my feet straight. I told them over and over again it was painful to do so, to which they responded by telling me that I had the lowest pain tolerance they'd ever seen. Thus, when visiting the last pediatrician I had seen, they had asked the doctor to tell me that I should walk with my feet forward.

"[Deadname] likes to listen to doctors rather than his parents," my mother said disapprovingly.

The doctor frowned, looked at my legs. The frown deepened.

"Well, I hate to say it, but he's right," the doctor said, referring to me. The doctor showed my parents that my tibia was badly twisted, resulting in my right leg being longer than my left and my right foot swinging outward when I walked.

"He can't walk straight. He physically can't. This would need to be fixed first," the doctor concluded, and handed my parents a referral to an orthopedic surgeon. The doctor then asked to see me without my parents present, having been clued in that something was wrong by their attitude and the red marks on my back. My mother refused, took my hand, and we left. I'm not entirely sure why my mother took me to the orthopedic surgeon, but he repeated what the pediatrician had said, and recommended a surgical device to untwist my offending leg. The doctor warned that without the procedure, not only would the problem get worse, but I would be in pain for the rest of my life, and eventually could lose the ability to walk altogether.

My mother flatly refused. She was not spending that kind of money on her lazy arrogant disappointment of a firstborn child, she said. I did not return to a doctor until I was well into my teenage years. My tibial torsion was never fixed.

It's not that my parents did not believe in doctors *ever*. A year later, when Sabrina injured her wrists from over-practicing piano, my parents got her physical therapists and a hand specialist from Johns Hopkins University in Baltimore. My mother herself was later diagnosed with Multiple Sclerosis, and my father had a team of doctors for her. The difference, my mother explained, was that she and Sabrina had earned it. I had not. And besides, perhaps the pain from my slowly tearing ligaments would make a man of me. My father and I would play catch in the backyard, with my father urging me to run through the pain of my degenerating knee and prove my worth. It was futile, of course; my torsion made me slow in addition to the pain, and there was no way to will myself to be faster, despite my best efforts. My father would say before each ball he'd hit to me, "How badly do you want it?"

When I inevitably would come up a step or two short, his next words would hit me like a sack of baseballs:

"I guess not that badly, huh?"

Yet what I found was that the pain was having the opposite effect. For the next several years, my weight fluctuated violently as I went through bouts of nausea followed by violent episodes of vomiting and diarrhea. My mother insisted I was faking it for attention, trying to substitute the care of doctors for the lectures on how I needed to stop being gay. The skin on my lip began to slough off weekly, which to my parents was a sure sign I was simply picking at it in an attempt to give myself cancer for sympathy. They even had their friend, a dentist, show me pictures of the cancers they thought I was attempting to give myself. When I protested that the skin was sloughing off, that the pain and nausea were real, I was ignored.

In reality, I was experiencing the early symptoms of what I would learn in adulthood was Crohn's Disease, an autoimmune condition. An autoimmune disease happens when the body's immune system confuses its own organs and tissues with foreign invaders and attempts to attack and reject them; in Crohn's, the attacks are focused on the intestinal tract, joints, and skin. Crohn's was also responsible for the damage to my knee that caused the torsion. But I of course did not know this then, and it would be more than a decade before I was diagnosed. The disease, of course, wouldn't wait around.

———

AROUND THIS TIME, my parents moved us from the congregation in Frederick to a far more observant Lubavitch congregation outside Baltimore. My mother told me this was because the Frederick congregation was too liberal and not Jewish enough, and she needed the assistance of real Jews to help to make me not gay; to her, real Jews supported Israel and the Republican party uncritically. However, that was, in truth, a rather charitable version of events. In reality, my mother had publicly told the entire congregation that a fellow teacher was engaged in an extramarital affair. The resulting fallout led to the Rabbi writing an op-ed in the shul paper calling my mother "bombastic," which my mother did not appreciate. The irony was that she had herself spent much of the previous year openly flirting with the father of one of her students, which she barely attempted to hide from me and hid from her other students not at all. When the man believed she was interested in a relationship and met her at her car, my mother told my father that she had no idea who he was.

The Lubavitch shul was a perfect choice for my parents because, like many ultra-orthodox synagogues, it was sex segregated. That meant I was required to be only with boys. My mother encouraged me to befriend the oldest son of the Rabbi to learn from him how to be a Jewish man, especially as I approached my Bar Mitzvah (the Jewish coming of age ceremony at age 13). I had no such interest. I'd started to become aware of the changes happening in my body, and they were literal torture. Each day I recognized my body less. Being reminded that this was something I would be forced to undergo simply wasn't something I was interested in. If I couldn't be a girl, maybe I could be a boy forever; becoming a man was simply not an option for me. So I befriended the younger kids instead. I regressed, spending more and more time with the stuffed owl I had slept with since birth, stubbornly refusing to grow up by sheer force of will.

My mother was incensed. To her, this proved her worst fears: that my gay "phase" was simply a result of immaturity and laziness. One day, she simply took away my owl and forbade me from sleeping with it. The next, she banned me from watching, playing, or discussing baseball or *Star Trek*. The forthcoming months, she said, would be spent solely on work. And work I did.

There was always, in truth, plenty of work to do on the farm. My parents had purchased for $4,000 a Massey Ferguson tractor with a front loader attachment a couple of years earlier; though it was decades old by that point, the bright yellow paint still gleamed in the sun. Early on, my father would let me ride it when my mother wasn't around, but over time, the tractor fell into disuse, and later disrepair. After all, my parents had purchased the tractor for spreading lime or seed in the fields, or turning over compost, or lifting hay bales – jobs which would take the tractor a matter of minutes. Yet my mother's insistence on giving those jobs to me instead meant that the tractor was off limits, lest it defeat the purpose of the exercise. Thus, the tractor sat in the largest field, unused, weeds sprouting up around it, as I walked around the field with a hand spreader filled with lime or seed. I turned one of the compost piles with a shovel, a job that took hours or days by hand, as the tractor's giant bucket, which could have scooped half the pile at once, sat silently on the ground. My mother would sometimes let me use the smaller Craftsman riding mower to mow fields in hours that would have taken the large tractor a few minutes, but sometimes she insisted I mow them by hand instead. She ordered me to pull poison ivy and poison sumac with my bare hands over and over again, telling me I needed to learn to bear the itch and pain like a man. I scratched anyway, unable to resist the itching, and as a result she and my sisters *also* got poison ivy rashes, for which she blamed me.

So much work was assigned to me that the tractor would sit unused for months or even years at a time. My father would periodically trek out to the old machine, clean out the birds' nests, lubricate the cylinders seized from water infiltration and stagnation, and eventually coax the engine back to life again. Yet there it sat, day after day, month after month, year after year, unmoving, a monument to my Sisyphean existence.

Still, I stubbornly refused to grow up, as though I could stop the process of puberty by sheer force of will. By throwing a full-on tantrum, I publicly embarrassed my mother into buying a lamp at a thrift store with a picture of a train on the shade; the lamp was clearly meant for younger children, even toddlers, but to me it was a symbol of my refusal to accept manhood. My father, upon seeing the lamp, was furious, and replaced the shade with a patternless one of a solid color.

Meanwhile, my mother was thoroughly enjoying her time at the Lubavitch congregation. My mother, a lifelong chameleon, easily switched between a genuine sounding country/western accent around town in Mount Airy and a more conventional mid-Atlantic accent around other people, but now added a more traditional Yiddish like cadence to her voice at this congregation.

I found the switching terribly confusing, and one day, whilst cleaning the horse stalls in the barn with my sisters, told them as much. It was very strange to me that our mother suddenly sounded so much like the Rabbi's wife when she had never sounded like that before. After talking it over with my sisters, I resolved to speak with our mother about it. Thus, after the stalls were finished, I did just that.

I had never seen my mother so furious. She ordered my sisters out of the room, and then, in what would be the final act of defiance of my childhood, I asked her point blank how there could be something wrong with me for being a girl unless there was also something wrong with her for changing how she talked based on who she was.

"You would turn my own children against me? Are you that much of an abomination, are you so desperate to put your penis in another man, that you would poison my own children, my pride and joy, against me? What did I ever do to you to deserve this treatment?"

I was confused. I was scared. And then she told me that she wished that I had been miscarried, that she wished the son she had actually miscarried had been born, that I was the worst thing to ever happen to her.

And then she told me to sit down in my chair at the kitchen table. Not knowing what was to happen next, I obeyed. She opened the pantry, pulled out a large gallon-size bottle of white vinegar, and wet a cloth with it.

"Open your mouth," she demanded, as she placed the cloth over my nose. The open bottle of vinegar in her left hand began to pour onto the cloth.

THE AMERICAN ACADEMY of Child and Adolescent Psychiatry defines "conversion therapies" as "interventions purported to alter same-sex attractions or an individual's gender expression with the specific aim to promote heterosexuality as a preferable outcome."[i] Merriam Webster's Dictionary defines it as "the use of any of various methods (such as aversive stimulation or religious counseling) in an attempt to change a person's sexual orientation to heterosexual or to change a person's gender identity to correspond to the sex the person was identified as having at birth."[ii] My mother had long been a proponent of conversion therapy, as Schlessinger was, believing that queer identities were conscious choices that could be trained and indoctrinated. If that were true, her thinking went, it logically followed that a queer identity could be *de*trained.

The popular narrative is that conversion therapy doesn't work. Popular media depicts conversion therapy as performed by quack doctors or pseudoscientific practitioners operating practices like any other mental healthcare provider. But there are caveats to this. Conversion therapy *is* effective – not at making a person less gay or trans, because that's impossible – but rather at breaking a person. The torturous effects of the practice break a person down inside, turn them against themselves. It doesn't make a person less queer. But it does make a person depressed, hopeless, and therefore pliant and easily controllable.

Thus a cottage industry has long existed of parents using the same methods on their children at home, especially among conservative parents who distrust medical professionals. Unsurprisingly, conversion therapy is no less pseudoscience, and no less harmful, when it's done by parents. A 2023 study[iii] found that parental conversion therapy was "associated with depression, suicidal thoughts, suicidal attempts, less educational attainment, and less weekly income." Yet despite this, there is little, if any, focus on people who undergo the practice at the hands of their parents. Thus, the popular conception of conversion therapy as a grift by professional snake oil salesmen is not incorrect, but it is incomplete.

My mother did not trust doctors. Thus, she didn't trust conversion therapy providers either. Instead, what she did to me, she did herself, using the same tactics, the same techniques. Sometimes, when he was home, my father would help her. It was not until years later that I identified it for what it was.

My mother would force me down onto a chair or the kitchen table, hold my nose shut, place a cloth over my face, and pour vinegar on the cloth as I gagged and writhed, unable to breathe, thinking I was drowning. Vinegar fumes would sting my nose and mouth; my eyes would water and I was never sure if they were tears from pain and sadness or simply irritation from the endless acidity of the vinegar. Undersized and skinny, I had no hope of struggling against my mother's grip, and after a while

I'd inevitably stopped trying, the futility of my resistance apparent.

I don't know how long each session lasted. I also don't know how many times she did it, though it was soon a regular occurrence outside the presence of my sisters. In the coming years, my mother would begin each of these sessions with the ironic phrase, "There's nothing wrong with mommy!" Whenever she would say it, I knew what was coming. My mother called these sessions "tough love," another term she appropriated from Schlessinger, who ironically enough also used the term to describe conversion therapy.

But in that first time at the kitchen table, as I gagged, after years of lectures and beatings, the center of calm finally collapsed. There was nothing there anymore when I went to search for it. There would be no more defiance, no more headstrong denials of rules, no more impulsiveness. In that moment, there was nowhere to run. The pain from the gagging was immense, but the greater pain was the helplessness, the utter pure helplessness as I felt the strength drain from my body. The only way to survive, I realized, was to not be a girl. But I could not *stop* feeling like a girl unless I stopped feeling everything. So I resolved in that moment to not feel anything at all. And for the next three years, I felt no joy, no rage, no happiness, no pain, not even despair. I felt only loss, the sense that I had once known who I was, but did no longer.

It had taken thirteen years, but she had won.

THE DARK TIMES

We are certainly damaged people. The question is, finally, do we use that damage, that first-hand knowledge of oppression, to recognize each other, to do what work we can together? Or do we use it to destroy?

— BARBARA SMITH

SIX

A few weeks after the first incident with the vinegar, my mother began charging me rent. I was 13 and had no money, but she was clear she'd have no faggot living for free under her roof. Perhaps naively, *still* not knowing what a faggot was, I had assumed my mother had given a similar ultimatum to my two sisters, and so I went to them, assured them no matter what I'd take care of them, that if necessary, we could leave together.

My mother was furious.

"I would never kick my children out of my house," she said, knowing fully well what the implication was for *my* relationship with her. "Just because I am kicking *you* out does not mean I am kicking my children out of the house. How dare you tell my children, make my children think, that I would ever do such a thing."

My mother set up a work schedule that would substitute for rent. When I completed the work, I was allowed to sleep in the house. I was too scared of what would happen if I did not "pay the rent" to test what would happen if I did not. I also barely cared.

I was a different person in the first half of my teenage years. I was robotic, unfeeling. It was not even that I did not feel so much as I could not feel; under the crushing weight of the vinegar on my face, I had simply switched my emotions off. Like the Vulcans I saw on *Star Trek*, I practiced suppressing my emotions to hide the pain. It wasn't just the pain of what my mother had done and would do again. It was my own utter revulsion with myself. I was revolted by my own surrender. I was disgusted by my slowly changing body, with male puberty beginning and my body feeling more foreign by the minute. I had internalized my mother's hatred for what I was. I despised the maleness of my body, and I hated myself for despising it, and I was disgusted with my helplessness. Rather than feel nothing but layers of self loathing, I opted to feel nothing at all.

When my mother asked me to do something, I did it without question. I let my mother write my bar mitzvah speech for me when she asked, something I would have been too proud to allow mere months earlier. Then I recited the speech the way she wanted, added the inflections and emphasis she wanted, where and when she wanted it. But when I read from the Torah and delivered the speech at the Lubavitch congregation, I felt nothing. The beautiful Hebrew words that had fascinated and enchanted me just a few months earlier when I gobbled up every Midrash and Talmudic volume I could find now induced no feeling whatsoever. Sick as a dog, having thrown up that morning, I watched myself read the words from above myself. There was inflection in their delivery, but it was the practiced emotional mimicry of a robot. It mattered little. She had wanted compliments and praise for my speech and performance from my parents' friends and other congregants, and she received them.

Years earlier, after watching the animated Disney movie *Pocahantas*, I had been so outraged by the racism and factual errors that I'd written to the studio, demanding a retraction; now, I cared so little for my schoolwork that I would leave pages unfinished. If my mother told me to do them again, I shrugged, completed the work, never really caring if the answer was right or wrong. I sided with my mother reflexively now, agreeing with her vociferously even where I knew she was wrong, *especially* where I knew she was wrong, parroting everything she said in the vein hope that maybe I could avoid the next session of vinegar. I was like a horse that had been broken. My mother told me I wasn't allowed to say anything at all to my sisters without asking her first. That set up a sadistic game for my mother wherein she would test my obedience by instructing me to make statements to my sisters threatening to hit them, or calling them names. If I complied, I was punished by a dressing down in front of them. If I refused, I was vinegared. I complied.

When Clint Black and a group of Christian Zionists held a rally for Israel's far right illegal settlement movement, I yelled racist slurs as loudly as my mother did at the counter protesters. My mother had long been a racist proponent of ethnic cleansing towards Palestinians, publicly advocating for their mass extermination. Just a year earlier, I had archly told my mother she was wrong that Palestinians were what she called an "invented people" based on my own research in the history books in the library, insisting it was actually Zionists, not Palestinians who were the intruders. Now, I no longer cared. I was watching someone else's life through my own eyes. Someone else was making these choices. My life did not belong to me. It belonged to her.

My mother took advantage of my complete surrender of my agency to her will to drive a further wedge between myself and my sisters, trying to further isolate me. One day, my mother instructed me to tell my sisters that if they ever picked on me or teased me, I would attack them.

"I want you to tell them that if they so much as look at you the wrong way, you will bring them down!" she ordered. I shrugged with my usual apathy, wanting the conversation to be over, and when my mother called in my sisters from playing outside, I did what she said. I remember thinking that maybe, if I got lucky, my mother wouldn't waterboard me this time. Only when I saw the horror on my sisters' faces did I realize the sadistic nature of the threat I'd just made. Maybe I was by that point too checked out of my own life to have realized the consequences. Maybe I was so programmed by that point that I simply obeyed without thinking. Or maybe I had realized it on some level but was too afraid of the consequences to even consider refusing. My mother feigned fury at the comment, of course, assured my sisters I would be duly punished, and lectured me in front of them for weeks thereafter. In private, however, she reminded me that if I refused, I would receive far worse than a lecture.

That wasn't the only shameful thing I did whilst wrapped up in my apathy. My mother ardently believed that Judaism was a race, and instructed my sisters and me as such. An ardent believer in Jewish racial purity, she railed frequently against intermarriage, and said that even converts weren't truly Jewish – a premise completely at odds with Jewish law. Still, for years I believed her. Partly this was because I had no other sources on the matter. After all, this was long before smartphones and the ubiquity of the internet. But also, my longtime apathy meant I simply didn't care; I would do whatever it took to avoid being waterboarded with vinegar. So, knowing my mother would read both, I therefore checked "other" in the race box for my applications for both college and law school. Only years later, in my early twenties, when I researched the origins of my mother's beliefs, did I realize just how wrong she – and I — had been. I eventually would shed my mother's Zionism, but it wasn't nearly soon enough.

For a while, my mother was thrilled. I was the obedient, unquestioning, obsequious child she'd always wanted. My father noticed the change in me, but was overtly torn about it. On the one hand, he did not want a queer child any more than my mother did. Yet on the other, as my mother responded to my ever increasing apathy with more and more draconian punish-

ments, each of which would lead to a period of greater acquies-
cence followed by even greater indifference, my father openly
wondered whether this was actually any better. Each night when
he arrived home at 1:00 am or 2:00 am in the morning, he would
wake me up, tell me about the Yankees game from the previous
night, and sometimes leave me a box score. And then he'd say,
"Don't tell your mother." Those small links with my father gave
me a glimmer of hope in the darkest time of my life.

Even in the face of my father's concern, my mother would
not be cowed, insisting that the brief periods of complete
surrender following each new session were proof that I was
capable of responsibility and manhood after all. Ironically, what
she took as me "trying" was exactly the opposite. I no longer had
any real ambition, because I no longer cared about my own life.
Neither of my parents believed in mental health care; my mother
often said, parroting Schlessinger again, that children being in
therapy or prescribed medications was simply a symptom of
parents not wanting to discipline their kids. "I bet that kid is on
Ritalin," my mother would say whenever she saw a misbe-
having child in public.

Besides, my Bar Mitzvah had been just a couple of months
after 9/11, and that gave my mother a convenient reason on
which to blame my clearly deepening depression. Flight 93 had
crashed two hours' drive from our house. Two hours the other
direction was the Pentagon, where my father frequented as an
audio engineer to set up the audio equipment for journalists
reporting stories from there on the evening news; had the attacks
been a week earlier, my father could have been among those
killed. Thus, rather than addressing the root cause, my mother
urged me to work out what she saw as the trauma of 9/11 by
building the twin towers out of Legos. I built the towers, and
then I tore them down, and still I felt nothing. My mother said
she was proud of me, that she loved me.

I lived to sleep, because the dreams never stopped. In my
dreams, I was still the girl I wanted to be. The platform in the

woods grew richer with each night, more branches, more leaves, more glitter. I would be dancing through the trees in pigtails, building forts of mud and sticks in my dress. There was just me and the butterflies and the birds. Then I would awaken, and it was gone, and I would go with it. I lived more in those dreams than I did in my waking hours.

I let Bucky step on my foot because I wanted to feel the pain. I fantasized about stabbing myself with a pitchfork, my punctured heart slowly beating to a stop. I opened the screen in my window, climbed out onto the awning, and wondered whether a fall from that height would kill me, too uncaring to actually do anything about it. It turned out that the son my mother always wanted was a daughter who was dead inside.

We left our synagogue shortly after that. My mother, never much able to keep herself from being the center of attention, caused quite a ruckus by publicly accusing a member of molesting his own daughter based solely on the fact that one day they came in with rumpled clothes. Leaving that congregation caused yet another grounding point in my life to become unmoored. Weekly trips to services were replaced by yard sale shopping, where my father would buy me used Legos to add to my growing collection.

Desperately seeking to hold onto some tiny facet of my identity, I spent day after day, week after week, month after month, sitting in my bedroom building with my Legos. Eventually, I started building what would become a fifteen foot long Lego starship model, with twenty-four decks, two shuttlebays, working turbolifts, a deflector dish, photon torpedo tubes, and quarters for a crew of a hundred and fifty. As I couldn't see color, I used whatever blocks were available, not bothering to make the floors or walls uniform if I couldn't see it anyway. Even building that ship, I felt nothing emotional but the compulsion to keep going; it became an obsession, as though my very life depended on its construction. Perhaps, not able to build myself the body that reflected my identity, I built the ship out of

Lego instead. Perhaps it was simply my mind rebelling at the cage it had been placed in. It was very likely the largest Lego starship model in the world by the time I finished college. It was far too big to take with me when I left, so it stayed behind, a silent rainbow behemoth, an ironic monument to the death of a childhood.

I have no idea what became of it.

For Sabrina, it could have been a grand time. My mother had spent years burnishing the competition between me and Sabrina – a competition I now essentially surrendered. From birth, I had a prodigious ability to read something once and recall it in its entirety; it may not have been an eidetic memory, but it was at least partially photographic. My mother considered this the source of my laziness, and often told Sabrina that the difference between her and I was that she actually works for and earns her grades, and I don't because of my memory. When Sabrina and I were in the same Hebrew School at the synagogue in Frederick, a tutor had asked how I learned Hebrew so quickly, and I had explained I simply visualized a flashcard with the Hebrew word on one side and the English on the other, arranged like icons on a computer desktop. My mother, believing I was attempting to show up Sabrina with what she called my "computer brain comment," spent hours at the kitchen table having me calculate multiplication of numbers. A slight smile on my face, I had spouted out answers faster than the calculator, only frustrating her more.

I used to take the competition seriously out of my own sheer pride. When Sabrina won a readathon by reading 230 books in a month to my 210, I resolved to win the next year and read 500 books just because I could. Now, though, I no longer cared. My mother told me Sabrina was smarter than me, more mature than me, more hardworking than me, and I simply agreed, as I did with everything else my mother said and did in those years. My sisters joked that I had no mind of my own.

"Of course you do," they'd say in practiced unison when I inevitably echoed my mother's opinion. My mother signed us up for karate lessons, and I deliberately stayed a half belt grade behind Sabrina so she would outrank me, just like my mother wanted.

Yet my mother hadn't wanted me to check out to such a degree that it left Sabrina without a flint on which to sharpen her own mettle. In that way, she'd actually overplayed her hand. Thus, she continued to urge a competition in which I simply had no desire to participate, having accepted my mother's statements as true that Sabrina was simply better.

"Are you really okay with not being as smart or responsible as your younger sister?" my mother would often ask.

"Yes," I responded indifferently.

Sabrina later told me that she was undergoing a different kind of pressure in those years: the pressure of not being outshone by someone who didn't even care about the competition anymore. She was, as it turns out, in her own kind of hell.

But what frightened my mother now about my ubiquitous apathy, moreso even than my abrogation of the competition with my sister, was how completely uninterested I was in male puberty. The terror I had long feared happening to my body was now years along, but the benefit of having checked out of my own life completely was that I felt dissociated from my own body. My reflection in the mirror now so little resembled myself that I would sometimes startle, wondering who was in the bathroom with me. Those changes belonged to someone else. I lived only in my dream life in the forest, and slept through the waking nightmare of my real life.

But to my mother, were I actually cured of the scourge of being gay, I would be acting more like a typical teenage boy than I was. One day, in a shoe store, my mother pointed out that another girl about my age was talking to me; I neither noticed nor cared. My mother signed me up for a homeschooling class with other students my age; a teenage girl my mother had pre-approved asked me out, and I said no. My mother tried to set me up with the daughter of a family friend, and I ignored it. At the state-required driving class for the written examination, a girl asked me out; I declined and simply said I had no interest in dating. My mother, aghast, noted she was "gorgeous" and asked if I was still gay.

My mother never did actually understand the issue; she did not understand the difference between being gay and being trans. It's true I'm attracted to men, but I always was primarily attracted to women. I'm bisexual, after all. But what my mother did not realize was sexual attraction to anyone from inside a *male* body was so utterly disgusting, an event so completely anathema to my identity, that it made me actively suicidal. It wasn't that I wasn't interested in women because I was inter-ested in men, it's that I couldn't imagine attraction to or interest in *anyone* in a body assigned male at birth because the physiolog-ical response was so entirely disgusting to me. To me, male geni-talia were a tumor, a foreign body, something that was as much naturally mine as a third arm.

I tried unsuccessfully cutting off my penis the first time I had an unintentional erection. Then I tried again. And again. Unable to sneak a knife out of the kitchen, I used any metal implement I could find, yet none was sharp enough, and the deepest I ever got was only about a half inch. When the cuts became infected, I had no choice but to show my father and ask for help; I lied that I had no idea where they came from. Whether or not he believed me, I will never know. I waited until they healed. And then I tried again. I would grab my testi-cles, twist them, twist them, twist them until the pain was unbearable, imagine twisting them until they fell off and I was free.

Yet my mother misinterpreted my apathy as evidence that I was still gay, and thus that her previous attempts had failed. So back to the vinegar she went, always without my sisters present. Back to the lectures she went. Her language became more brutal.

"Damn you to hell," she cried at me one time when a chicken escaped, convinced it was my gayness shining through.

"I wish you'd never been born," she spit another time, spraying insect killer in my face at the kitchen table after my sisters were asleep.

I stacked hay bales and cords of firewood, split logs, pulled yet more poison ivy. My mother would pull me out of bed after my sisters were asleep and talk to me, sometimes lecturing and sometimes beseeching, trying to impress upon me the importance of being a "red blooded American male" to the future of the family. One night, she tried a different approach.

"The rules are black and white," she said. "But life is gray. The rules say that you can't be gay, but maybe you have urges anyway. That's okay, just don't act on them. That's the gray part of life. As long as you don't act on them, I'll still love you."

The next day, she invoked that axiom again.

"The rules are black and white," she said. "But life is gray. The rules say that you never have sex before marriage, but maybe one day you're getting hot and heavy with someone really attractive and you do it anyway. That's okay. I'll still love you."

After years of being lectured, and beaten, and waterboarded with vinegar, after working myself past heat stroke over and over again, pulling poison ivy with my bare hands, I laughed noiselessly to myself, gave her the hug she requested, and went to bed.

BY THIS TIME, my mother had pulled us out of the intramural softball league as part of her latest attempt to punish me for my transness by removing baseball from my life. My mother long believed my borderline obsession with baseball to be related to my queerness. To her, baseball was a sign of my laziness, and thus she often would bar me from having anything to do with baseball, preferring I work in the fields instead. Of course, I still needed a physical education class, so as a teenager my mother signed the three of us up for a homeschool bowling league at an alley forty five minutes away in Frederick.

To everyone's surprise, most of all my own, it turned out I was good. And not good by the standards of the homeschool league I was in, either. I was legitimately, actually *good*. The first season, autumn, I averaged over 130, best in the league. The second season, after my father bought me a bowling ball at a yard sale, I pushed my average to over 160, again the best in the league. When my average hit 180 that summer, a coach at the bowling alley started giving me pointers, and told my parents I could legitimately consider bowling as a potential career path with the proper training. What made my success strange was how unconventional it was; unlike most bowlers, who threw the ball with a hook to meet the pins in the pocket, I threw my thirteen-pound ball straight as an arrow into the pocket, with surprising accuracy. I was so good, in fact, that by the end of the summer I was drawing crowds of strangers watching me, which was unnerving every time; I'd bowl typically well until I realized I was being watched, and then promptly fall apart completely.

At fourteen, my parents signed me up for a series of semiprofessional tournaments around the state. My first appearance, I was so nervous that I rolled three consecutive gutter balls to start the game, which essentially cost me any chance at finishing on the podium. With no pressure left on me and everyone having moved on to the more interesting matches, I bowled a strike every single remaining frame in the game. My father was the only one watching by the end, but he was proud of me.

"You really looked like a professional up there," he said to me, with real pride in his eyes. My mother was less gracious, upset that my slow start had cost her the prize money. I did fairly well at the various tournaments, finishing in the middle of the pack, but my mother was unwilling to pay for lessons or coaching unless I actually won a tournament. The coach at the Frederick alley was still convinced I had a future in the sport, but it was not to be. That is, to this day, for me the road not taken. I have no idea if I could have made a real go of it, but in the last league game I ever played, as a fifteen-year-old, I bowled over 250.

Around this time, my father decided he'd had enough of the F-150 as a daily driver. As a farm truck, it was outstanding, capable of hauling pretty much anything and splashing through the mud in the fields to deliver hay and straw and bags of feed. But it was ill-suited to my father's increasingly lengthy commute.

Mount Airy was not the tiny town it was almost a decade earlier. A Weis Markets had expanded from a convenience store to a full-blown supermarket, and shortly thereafter a Super Fresh market moved in with a strip mall next to it. Then came the Food Lion, and a year later a Walmart. By this time the post office was out of its since-destroyed strip mall and in a new, modern building, and Mount Airy even had five intersections fully controlled with stoplights now. What had been a tiny dot where everyone had to drive to Damascus twenty minutes away to get food was now where people from Damascus came to do *their* shopping. One of the largest farms in the town was sold to developers, and then a second, and then a *third*, and the town grew from less than a thousand people to almost five times that in less than a decade. More people meant more traffic, and more traffic meant a longer commute, and now my father was spending nearly two hours in the truck one way between the farm and WRC. Worse, all of the attributes that made the truck an awesome hauler also made it abysmal on fuel economy. So, one day, my father came home with a 1998 Pontiac Bonneville. It was a mid-tier SLE trim, with leather heated seats, digital climate control, and the venerable Series II Buick 3800 V6 engine that made a smooth, distinctive hum as it accelerated down the interstate, and I loved it on sight.

My father had long loved General Motors cars in general and Pontiac in particular. He'd never cared much for foreign cars, especially German ones, though he had owned a Toyota Celica before I was born. He would spend hours telling me of the importance of buying American cars, though before the Bonneville arrived I hadn't really internalized his words. Like many teenagers, I dreamed about a car of my own, though my own sensibilities tilted more toward, as Nissan called it in the television commercials I saw, the Nissan Maxima "Four-Door Sports Car." All of that changed the first time I sat in "Bonnie," however. I felt strangely drawn to her, as though a piece of myself had been linked to that car. I didn't yet know it, but Bonnie would one day be my chariot to freedom.

SEVEN

Note: This chapter contains graphic details of sexual abuse.

Until I was a teenager, my mother believed solely in abstinence to a degree Schlessinger would be proud of. Yet as the complete apathy of my dissociative depression stretched into my fourteenth and then fifteenth years, my mother became increasingly alarmed. I would absent-mindedly parrot back my mother about literally everything. I slept as often as I could, not because I was tired, but because in the forest, as *the girl* in the forest, I was actually alive, unlike the waking death of my real life.

And so my mother decided to take more drastic actions.

My mother started by urging my sisters to tease me about every woman on television they could think of, telling them (falsely) that I had a crush on them. There were a couple that were true – Kirsten Dunst's Mary Jane Watson was among my first crushes ever – but in truth the physiological reaction to them was so profoundly negative that I desperately tried not to think about it. My mother's tactic here was thus literally torturous, forcing me to think about that physical reaction *all the time,* and my entreaties to stop were ignored. My mother's evening talks became less lectures and more outright gaslighting, telling me that my sisters were right to tease me because I must really have crushes on those women.

One real crush I did have was on a sportscaster at my father's television station, a pretty blonde woman in her 20s. Left to my own devices, I would have done nothing about it. But my mother, seeing an opportunity, saw her walking down a hallway one day and asked me to get her a glass of water from the drinking fountain. I had no idea she was walking towards me. Once again, I had the normal physiological reaction. When I ducked into the bathroom, my mother and sisters erupted in laughter, thinking I was embarrassed. In reality, I was throwing up. I was searching for something, anything, to get that cursed appendage off of my body, an appendage that belonged as much to me as to a Martian. I was attracted to her, but *as a bisexual woman*.

"It's normal for a teenage boy. You might just be a normal red blooded American male after all, thank G-d," she said. But I did not *feel* normal. I felt nauseous, all the time, would spend hours in the basement bathroom throwing up, day after miserable day. Night after night I would go to bed praying that G-d either let me wake up a girl or not wake up at all. And morning after morning I would wake up, cry, and feel nothing else.

My MOTHER'S best friend at the time was also our veterinarian, Karen. Tall, slim, and blonde, and about my mother's age, when she wasn't caring for animals, she was part of a rock band. She'd sometimes come over for dinner with her boyfriend, and my mother hatched a plan to use her to awaken what she still thought was my slumbering sexuality. To this day, I don't know if Karen was in on it or not. I only know what my mother did.

Karen was holding a fundraising concert for the fake animal rescue my mother ran out of the farm. The concert was held at a proper venue, and thus the performers all had dressing rooms. My mother wrote something down on a piece of paper, gave it to me, and instructed me to find Karen in her dressing room and give it to her.

"And whatever you do," my mother said, looking at me with those cold eyes. "You are *not to knock*."

Three years earlier, I would have knocked anyway, because it was the right thing to do. Three years earlier, I would not have cared what my mother instructed. But the day before I had been vinegared again. I was, in all candor, simply not thinking clearly enough to understand the implications of what I was being told to do. It didn't make it right – as a fourteen or fifteen years old (I don't remember which), I *should* have realized. But the truth was that I was simply going through the motions obediently, waiting for the day to be over, and without thinking at all, did exactly what I was told.

Karen was naked.

Startled, I mumbled a profuse apology, dropped the note, and ran. I ran out of the dressing rooms, out of the backstage area, out of the *building*. I ran until my legs no longer carried me.

And then I threw up, the full implications of what had just happened – of what *I had just done* – hitting me with full force. I knew I couldn't ask my mother what to do next, so I figured the safest thing to do would be to ask my father. I searched the building for him. But I couldn't find him until after the show, and that meant my mother found me first.

In my mother's version of events, I hadn't run because I had just barged into someone's dressing room unannounced. Oh no. In my mother's version of events, I had run because I was gay, because naked women scared me, *and that meant I had failed her test*.

Karen was only interested if I was okay, having heard my

mumbled apology and seen me make the hastiest exit in the history of the venue, and concerned for me. But my mother dismissed her concerns and said this was an ongoing issue with me that they'd discuss with me later.

By "discuss," my mother meant more vinegar.

Also at the concert was the first trans person I'd ever met, a trans woman performer named Georgia. I found her fascinating. I didn't know what transitioning was, of course, but something about Georgia reminded me of me. My mother was quick to put her foot down, calling Georgia an abomination and instructing us to only refer to her using male pronouns "since he's a gay man." (This confused me very much, as Georgia was married to a woman. When I asked my mother to explain, she said that this kind of "living in sin" is "common with perverts" and failed to elucidate, which only confused me more.)

Then one day, my mother held a family meeting, at which she said that I had something to tell everyone. She said that I would be talking about what had been "bothering" me. In retrospect, my mother probably wanted me to tell the family I was a gay abomination. Instead, I mustered up what little was left of my courage, and said "I have a problem with how we're treating Georgia."

My mother's mouth dropped open. I continued.

"You say [s]he's an abomination, and obviously I agree because you're obviously right, you're always right, but um, why then is it okay to take [her] money?"

My mother responded – at least, in front of my father and sisters — that this was our way of providing penance for Georgia for her lifestyle of sin, and that by helping the rescue she could be redeemed through good deeds. But later that night, she pulled me aside.

"I want to make something very clear. No amount of charity will ever redeem *my* son from being an abomination like that. Not *my* son. You become like him, you're dead to me, dead to your father. We sit shiva for you. We bury your casket. Do you understand me?"

MY MOTHER'S plan with Karen having failed, she next tried a more direct approach. One day, with my father at work, she told me to bring up the laundry basket from the laundry machines in the basement and put the folded clean laundry on my parents' bed. It was a typical chore, so downstairs I went. My parents' door was closed when I arrived upstairs, but I had been through this before, so this time I knocked. Loudly.

"Come in," said my mother.

"Are you sure?" I said, wanting to be *absolutely certain this time.*

"I said, come in," she said sternly. So I opened the door.

In retrospect, it was largely predictable that my mother was standing naked next to her dresser. Still, to my teenage self, it was a gut punch. I closed the door, apologized, and when my mother called after me, I ignored her. But from then on, my mother would come over and whisper in my ear, "Are you touching yourself? Are you touching your penis?"

My mother told me she did this in an attempt to arouse me so that I would be attracted to women. She believed, having (according to her) studied psychology in college, that being gay could be cured by the latent attraction all assigned male at birth people feel for their mothers. It goes without saying that this did not work.

I NEVER TOLD my father most of what is in this chapter. My father idolized my mother, though their relationship began under what can only be considered to be unacceptable circumstances given the age difference. And it's certainly possible, if not plausible, that played a role – perhaps an outsized one – in how she treated me.

My father could be tender, loving, even openly supportive, in ways my mother never was. He was openly complimentary to my mother and never laid a hand on her. He only hit the three of us when instructed to do so by my mother. My mother also would routinely hit him, denigrate him, tell him he was insufficient and brag that she could do better. She would even, at times, encourage us to do the same, urging us to punch our father in the stomach for fun. Our home revolved around her; she was the central force in all of our lives. My father was utterly devoted to her, called her the love of his life, swore fealty to her the way a knight would kneel before a monarch.

Early after my escape, I thought of my father as the "good" parent and my mother as the "bad" one. Yet at the same time, this reality that I saw with my own eyes, of a dominant woman, abusive towards her husband, abusive to me, and later abusive to my youngest sister Elaina, is difficult to reconcile with what I know to be the origins of my parents' relationship. The age gap, the murkiness around when they started dating, that the three of us never met anyone in my mother's family growing up, speak to the very real possibility that my mother was groomed by my father.

Did the power imbalance in my parents' relationship switch at some point? Or was there more going on behind the scenes between my parents than what I was privy to? Perhaps both are true. Perhaps my father groomed my mother but also genuinely did love her. Perhaps he groomed her *because* he loved her. Regardless, what happened between my parents undoubtedly informed how they each interacted with me as I grew up, and as their fears that I was queer became more fully realized. If my mother was to be believed, by the time she was 15, she and my father were already "together." As I write this, at 36 years old, I am almost 15 years older than my mother was at the time my parents married, and yet still younger than my father was. When my mother was 36, I was already a teenager. When my father was 36, he was unmarried with no children.

Thus my mother's view of sex and sexuality had been skewed through no fault of her own. Would she have viewed any of what she did to me as acceptable absent what my father did to her? I don't know. Would my father even have objected had he known? Perhaps, in retrospect, she and I were both victims of my father. For years, I resolved I would never be my mother, simply because I saw her as the epitome of evil for sexualizing me at an age where not only was I incapable of consenting, but in a place where I had no ability whatsoever to meaningfully object. Not until much later, when I was in my 30s, did I come to realize the parallels – incapacity to consent, inability to object – between what she did to me and in her own "relationship" with my father. It does not excuse what she did. It does not absolve her. But it does demonstrate the degree to which trauma can pass, unaddressed, through and between generations.

There are also those who will read this book and conclude that it was what happened in this chapter that made me trans, that I am simply remembering incorrectly and that my transness is the result of sexual abuse. They would be wrong. I do not know if what my mother did to me was truly out of an attempt to de-trans me, or whether it was her attempt to process her own trauma. Maybe it was the latter and she told herself the former. There was, of course, a deeply bitter irony in queerness being my parents' deepest fear for their children, given the origins of their relationship. Yet the truth remains that there is a dividing line in my memory, clear as day. Before I came out to my parents, before Jane, I was the headstrong, impulsive, disobedient child.

"I love you," my mother would say in those days, "but I don't like you very much."

It wasn't exactly heartwarming, but it was affection nonetheless. I was a disappointment, but I was a disappointment as a result of my own obstinacy.

After I came out, however, I became something else. If before I was a disappointment if only because I was so constantly exasperating, afterwards I became something more, something dangerous. I was a black mark for my parents, something they were ashamed of, a disgrace to be hidden away and kept from public view. My mother stopped referring to me as one of her children, instead using "my children" to refer to Sabrina and Elaina and "you" to refer to me. She'd openly ask G-d in front of me what she'd done to be punished with me, and whether she really deserved the shame I brought upon her. On her birthday, on holidays, she would mutter "Happy birthday to me" to herself sarcastically as I walked by – not congratulating herself, but bemoaning her ill fortune of being cursed with my presence on what should have been a day of joy. I was some kind of sick joke played on her by the universe.

My childhood cannot be separated from the origins of parents' relationship for another reason as well. My father, deeply patriarchal, often said that having his oldest child be a son was the proudest moment of his life, and my mother considered having a son to be her highest duty as a wife. That I turned out to be, well, *not* a son, that I rejected utterly the great "honor" that I was supposed to be, was something they viewed not unlike spitting in their faces. I know this because they told me as much. I was supposed to be the culmination of their relationship, the son who made their relationship worth it and justified what they saw as their sacrifices: my father going against his parents' wishes to marry my mother, my mother leaving behind her entire family. Instead, not only did I eschew the role entirely, I did so with no substitute, no replacement; there was no other son to, as my parents put it, "carry on the family name."

But what was even worse for my parents was the fact that from their perspective, I wasn't terribly good at being a girl, either. I was perfectly happy to be a tomboy, playing with Legos, building things. Sabrina was graceful, musical, beautiful, deliberate. I was, in many ways, her opposite. What scared my parents even more than my insistence I was a girl was the kind of girl I would be: one completely untethered by the conservative gender norms around which they had built their entire relationship.

I was a teenage trans girl. And so, I was an existential threat to my parents' entire world. At that time, I just had absolutely no idea why.

EIGHT

My parents insisted every Halloween on donating half the candy the three of us received each year Trick-or-Treating to the kids in the pediatric ward at the local county hospital. In truth, it was a beautiful tradition. One Halloween, whilst the three of us were trick-or-treating with my mother, a lesbian couple answered the door in one of the new developments that had been popping up around Mount Airy. My mother, of course, lectured them about how inappropriate it was for them to be around children. The two women, who had done nothing but offer us candy, were too surprised to say anything in the face of such an unexpected onslaught. My mother, taking that as a victory, said "come on guys, their candy isn't good for us," and ushered us away. From then on, we avoided their house on Halloween.

My mother was gravely concerned about the arrival of a lesbian couple in Mount Airy. She quizzed me multiple times if I had gone over to their house, which I had not, and which would have been impossible anyway. My denials actually made her more upset, because she could have understood and accepted if I was gay because of *them*. Being queer because of being "born that way" was a threat to my mother's entire worldview, and she continued to believe that I had somehow been made gay by them even though they had just moved into town, *years after we had*.

My mother was desperate at this point to awaken any kind of sexuality in me, and finally instructed me that I had a crush on my sister Sabrina. This prompted very public teasing by Elaina, who at five years younger than me did not understand the gravity of what was happening. I could have, *should have* refused to comply with my mother's demand. Yet I was still sleep-walking through life, trying anything to just get through the day. If my mother had told me to walk into the sea, I would have done so.

What was even worse was that the vinegar sessions, the lectures, the reminders that she wished I'd never been born, all happened anyway. I saved myself nothing by hurting my sisters. By this point, I was probably strong enough that I could have fought back. But I had simply no desire to do so. Where would I go, anyway? My mother had ensured a wedge had been driven between myself and my sisters such that our relationship was, at best, frayed. We were on a farm in the middle of nowhere. I went through the motions, ending every day praying not to wake up, hoping that G-d would let me die whilst in the forest where I belonged, and beginning every morning feeling nothing at all.

MY PARENTS BEGAN LOOKING for houses again, this time even farther out.

My mother had her heart set on a massive property in central Pennsylvania, a two and half hour drive from my father's work. The real estate agent, when asked if the neighborhood had a problem with Jews, scoffed and said "Oh please. It's not as if you're Black." My mother approved, and since my father did whatever my mother wanted, so did he.

I had no desire to move. I wasn't at all *happy* where we were, but I also knew that another move would probably end whatever few guardrails remained on how my mother treated me. At the time, Pennsylvania had homeschooling laws more lax even than Maryland's once-every-six-months check-in with a representative of the county. So I admittedly cast about for a way to scuttle the sale. Then at the final pre-purchase inspection, I noticed a water line on the outside of the house.

The plot in question had a house and two outbuildings, all surrounding a central pond. A quick check revealed a similar water line on the other two buildings, so I went over to the real estate agent, brought my father with me, and asked "Does this property ever flood?" The agent denied it, so I showed my father the water lines. My father asked the real estate agent to check, to which my mother objected, but my father didn't want to take out a mortgage on a flood property. It turns out the property did flood, quite frequently in fact, and that was the reason for the sale in the first place. My father wasn't willing to buy the property anymore.

Soon after, when I was 15, my mother's second worst nightmare came true behind me being gay: A Black family moved in next door. I use "next door" loosely, because Mount Airy wasn't exactly known for houses that were close together, least of all *farms*. But the house closest to ours now was home to a Black family.

My mother, of course, blamed me, which she constantly reminded me.

"I will never, *ever* forgive you for costing me my dream home and making me live next to… THOSE PEOPLE," she would say, over and over again, at home, in stores, at the barn, in the horse stalls.

As it turned out, one of "those people" saved my life. The family consisted of a couple and their six kids, and their oldest, Darryl, was a year older than me. And I was instantly drawn to him for the simple fact that unlike me, he wasn't afraid of my mother.

It took Darryl all of ten seconds to size up my mother. When she forbade him from speaking with me, he would appear to leave, wait until she'd left the vicinity of the front door, and sneak me out of the house anyway. When she would tell him I wasn't allowed to go play catch with him, he'd wait, hiding in the bushes, until I came out. He and his brothers would take me and a group of friends with them to the little baseball field at the park a mile away, where we'd play five-on-five scrimmages, field ground balls, take batting practice. And when my mother was busy, he and I would play in our backyard.

It was Darryl who cracked a bit of sunlight into the apathy that had become my life. My first time at the ballfield with him and his brothers, I felt something besides numbness for the first time in years. The first time a groundball was hit to me, I laughed. Not a chuckle, either: a full-on, side splitting belly laugh. Not because fielding a ground ball is funny (though watching me trying certainly is), and not even because of nerves, but because I had forgotten what it felt like to be happy, and this was happiness, and in that one moment I lived a thousand lifetimes.

Darryl didn't understand this, of course. He didn't know why I was laughing, and looked at me with a truly quizzical expression, saying "It's not that funny, man!" And of course he didn't know my secret; he didn't know I was trans, or anything about my mother beyond her extremely obvious racism. As far as he was concerned, I was the kid of the racist bitch next door. But he saved my life, even if he didn't realize it. He taught me about football and hitting – seriously, he was the best hitter I'd ever seen up close, he could have gone pro if he'd wanted. But mostly he was the first person since I was in kindergarten who thought I mattered.

"The key to not getting in trouble is not getting caught," he'd say about my mother with a glint in his eye.

MY MOTHER HAD by this point resolved to enlist me in the military. She'd been threatening me with military school for a while, but by now had decided that wouldn't be enough.

"I've done my best," she'd say. "Maybe they can make a man out of you."

Each year, my mother administered to each of us the California Achievement Tests, a standardized test to determine our grade level aptitudes in various subjects. Though my mother didn't tell me until much later, I had tested at a college level before my thirteenth birthday, and the county reviewer had wanted me to go. Despite this, my mother had no expectations for me going to college. Quite frankly, she said, I was too lazy and too much of a disappointment to warrant the expense.

"It takes much more than just smarts," she told the county reviewer, "and he doesn't have what it takes."

If I wanted to go to college, I would need a scholarship, and the middling grades she'd given me the previous few years on what would be my homeschooling equivalent of a high school transcript made the prospects of *that* bleak at best. To be fair, I had not exactly been trying my best during those years. I saw no reason to.

But the prospect of joining the military scared the shit out of me. I wasn't at all scared of dying – by this point, I was praying to die every night. I was, however, terrified of hurting someone else. So my mother signed me up for the PSAT and SAT, a month apart, and we made a deal: If I didn't get a scholarship, I would let her enlist me. Darryl and I decided in secret to apply to the same colleges. But when I got my PSAT scores back, they were average.

I didn't sleep at all the night before the SAT. And then, sleep deprived, having thrown up the previous day's meals, fueled by nothing but adrenaline and fear, at 15 years old I scored in the 99th percentile in the state on the SAT.

It was, in all honesty, a fluke. It was lucky. It was *beyond* lucky. Darryl – who was far, far smarter than I was – didn't score nearly that well. I got two scholarship offers: Catholic University in DC offered me a full scholarship, and McDaniel College offered me 80% off tuition. My mother's tune changed; she suddenly went from saying that I lacked the ambition and skillset to go to college, to praising my score as a vindication of her teaching methods. She'd been able to get even me into college. I would be just 16 when I started, so my mother chose the college for me: Catholic University would require me to live on campus, so my mother selected McDaniel, just twenty minutes from where we lived. Within the span of day, I went from my mother itching to kick me out so I could join the military and she could be rid of me, to my mother requiring me to live at home so she could keep an eye on – and, in all candor, bask in the media attention and take credit for — the sixteen year old wunderkind who'd be the youngest person in their college class by over a full year.

And so, for the first time in over a decade, I was headed to a classroom. I had no idea what that meant, but I thought it beat the hell out of joining the military. That is, until I learned that Darryl *hadn't* gotten a scholarship. His parents, unlike mine, weren't wealthy. He *did* have to join the military.

By all rights, if the world was a just and fair place, my spot at McDaniel should have gone to him. He was smarter than me. He was more athletic than me. He was a better person than me. I got a better score on one standardized test. I got the scholarship. He went to Iraq. I never saw him again.

ROCK BOTTOM

Damaged people are dangerous. They know they can survive.

— JOSEPHINE HART

NINE

Sixteen year olds being students on college campuses is a rare enough phenomenon that before I arrived, professors in the classes I signed up for received a letter from the administration warning them of my forthcoming arrival. It didn't take long for word to spread around campus, and thus by the time orientation arrived, people were already talking about the sixteen year old in the incoming first year class and who it might be. Given my mother picked me up and dropped me off every day – I did not yet have even a learner's permit, to say nothing of a driver's license — it didn't take a genius to realize that was me. Before the end of my first day of classes, I was being called a "freak," a "prodigy."

I hated it.

Admittedly, some of the schoolwork was less challenging than I had anticipated. I had spent years reading every book I could get my hands on, and so much of the material in my first year introductory classes was covering information I already knew. Yet this did nothing for my confidence. After years of having no friends besides Darryl – whom I'd only known for less than eighteen months — I had, in truth, no social skills to speak of. I didn't know how to have a conversation, and talking on the phone gave me panic attacks. I raised my hand for every question, because the last time I had been in a classroom was kindergarten and that's what I had done there.

But there was more to it than that. I didn't know how much my mother knew about what I was doing and saying in classes. My parents' condition for allowing me to go to college instead of enlisting was that I lived at home, and that meant I remained – at least in part – under her control. Every day, my mother would give me a list of lines I was allowed to use in response to what she saw as the liberal brainwashing of the professors. If there was a movie to be watched in class, she'd watch it first. If there was a textbook assigned, she had my father read it first. Any reading materials had to be brought home to be reviewed by my parents. I was required to memorize scripts of acceptable responses they'd written to the material. I was terrified of what would happen if I broke away from her lists of acceptable statements, so I hewed to them as closely as possible. I hadn't figured out if my professors would report my statements to my parents – after all, my mother had *said* they would – so I opted to err on the side of extreme caution.

At the same time, there was something legitimately liberatory about being away from that house, even if it was only for a few hours at a time. During that time, I knew I would be safe from the worst of my mother's wrath, even if only by a few miles. I was like a newborn mammal, eyes still closed, ears still closed, legs barely functional, not quite knowing where I was going, but going nonetheless.

My mother insisted that I give her a copy of every assignment I completed prior to handing it in to the professor. She was suspicious of professors, convinced that if they caught wind of what she called my "past homosexual tendencies" they would attempt to nurture them, and she would lose me. Dutifully, prior to turning in my very first college paper — in my first year philosophy class — I handed it to my mother; she gave it back an hour later with a list of changes and additions she wanted made, including, of course, citations to Schlessinger. I made her edits and handed in the paper.

A week later, I received the paper back. I had received a poor grade; the professor noted a nascent writing ability, but the various additions my mother had demanded had been surrounded by a sea of negative commentary in what I can only assume was red ink. Startled, I read the professor's notes again, and again, and *again*, as it dawned on me that *every single point deducted from the paper had been for a change demanded by my mother*

That evening, I showed the paper to my parents in the kitchen. My father was home from work that night and cooking dinner, and my mother leaned against a countertop reading silently, her brow furrowed. I waited silently to see if my mother reached the same conclusion I had. Rather predictably, she had not. Instead, my mother believed my poor grade was vindication for her unflattering assessment of my intelligence and work ethic, and roundly criticized me for choosing to go to college instead of enlisting.

"I'm never wrong, and you should have listened to me," she continued.

Yet by now I was only half listening to the lecture. I still remember the tiniest kernel of an idea, bouncing around my head, a question I dare not utter out loud: What if my mother isn't right about me? How much does she *actually* know? She had to be seeing the same criticisms I was, the same comments. The truth — that my mother had set me up to fail on purpose — wouldn't occur to me for years. Yet I now had evidence that my mother wasn't nearly as omnipotent as I had been treating her. The trick would be figuring out what to do about it.

"...so of course you'll be dropping out," I heard my mother say, bringing me out of my thoughts.

"Absolutely not," I said, with a conviction I thought myself no longer capable of. And then, without thinking, purely impulsively, I added, "And I'll be valedictorian when I graduate." I had surprised myself into silence. *Valedictorian? What, exactly, was I thinking?*

My father sighed, joining the conversation for the first time. "Stuey, I don't think you realize how hard that is. It's not easy being valedictorian, and we all know you don't love hard work, and there's no shame in listening to your mother."

But something inside me bristled at the implication, as though the little girl who had been asleep for years had begun to stir. And I repeated, more insistently, that I would be valedictorian. My parents never brought up dropping out again. And from then on, I did every assignment – every paper, every quiz, every essay – twice. One copy, I turned into my mother, awaited her feedback, and then discarded it. The other copy I actually handed into my professor.

I finished my first semester with straight As.

MY FIRST DAY of that same philosophy class, I met Kayla. A sophomore, she sat next to me in class. She introduced me to her brother, David, and he and I sat together in an art history class I took in my second semester. The three of us became fast friends, hanging out in the student union between classes and whilst I was waiting for my mother to pick me up.

Kayla and David were commuter students also, but at 19 and 20, they didn't have to wait for their parents to get them. Still, they treated me as an equal, which was a pretty rare thing. Most of the other students treated me either as a curiosity, a freak, or an annoying younger sibling.

For that reason, I loved spending time with them. They taught me to play poker, which we did with plastic chips because none of us had any money. David and I played chess and checkers. They shared my love of *Star Trek* and even told me about the episodes that my mother had forbidden me from seeing. For instance, they described to me the Next Generation's

Season 5 episode *The Outcast*, where guest star Melina Culea plays Soren, a member of a genderless species who grows up believing herself to be a woman and falls in love with Jonathan Frakes' Commander Riker. The parallels with my own life were, of course, obvious, and so I watched the episode in the student union on my laptop with headphones. The reason my mother had banned the episode from the house was clear, but it left me with more questions than answers. The J'naii, the alien race that forcibly returns Soren to her previous genderless form, seemed to closely resemble my mother. But weren't they the villains of the story?

My mother seemed to sense that I was being pulled towards my new friends, and was increasingly concerned about the new ideas I was expressing. She couldn't stop me from seeing them without simply following me around on campus everywhere, and I doubted she'd go that far. And when she started accusing me of sleeping with Kayla, I knew she'd overplayed her hand. Not only was it simply not true, I wouldn't have even known *how*; for all of my mother's repeated attempts to "make me a man," neither she nor my father had ever had a single conversation with me about the actual mechanics of having sex. With my extremely limited internet access and no cell phone – this was, after all, 2005 — I wouldn't have even known where to look to find out.

Thus, it didn't take me long to figure out that what bothered my mother wasn't that she thought Kayla and I were in a relationship. No, what bothered my mother was that she couldn't *control* whatever was happening between us. We were friends, nothing more, and in all candor I was relishing having multiple friends for the first time since Kindergarten. Every time I would arrive back in the car at the end of a school day, my mother was demanding to know if I had been hanging out with Kayla and David. Every time we'd arrive home, she'd berate me for disobeying her whilst I leaned against the wall in the kitchen, only half listening. A bit of my former willfulness was returning, and it felt like the high from a drug. And so, in the second semester of my first year, I decided to see just how far I could push things.

One day, I was playing poker with Kayla, David, and a couple of their other friends in the quad. My mother was an hour late picking me up, so when she finally arrived, I decided to finish playing the hand before leaving. It was, as acts of rebellion go, incredibly tame; my mother was waiting outside the quad for less than ten minutes.

It was ten minutes too long.

My mother did not stop screaming the entire drive home, reaching volumes I had not thought her capable of, making wilder and wilder accusations. By the time we arrived, she'd talked herself into a belief that Kayla and I had been mid-coitus when she arrived. My response – the truth, that we were playing a very ordinary game five card draw with plastic chips and I wanted to finish the hand – seemed only to anger her further. She decided that if Kayla was able to "corrupt" me so easily, she must have been trained somewhere, and obviously that must have been a cult. She had been reading about cults online, and she believed that Kayla was a representative of what she had been reading online about the "transgender cult."

Ironically, that was the first time I'd ever heard the word "transgender." Even in our discussions of Georgia, the word had never been used. I had no idea what it meant, so its significance went straight over my head. But in retrospect, my mother had believed Kayla would get me to transition. Kayla wasn't trans — both she and her brother were cis and straight – but my mother wasn't going to let facts get in the way.

Calmly I explained to my mother that no, they weren't in a cult, I wasn't in a cult, we were all just friends, and we had been playing poker. My mother was having none of it. The argument went on for hours until finally my mother played her ace, the one thing she had that I couldn't do a damn thing about.

"Either you admit everything or you get out of my house

tonight. And I don't mean the barn. You can live somewhere else."

From the tone of her voice I knew she was serious, especially when she took my clothes and started putting them in a garbage bag. Kayla and David lived in Pennsylvania, two hours away by the car I didn't have. *I had nowhere else to go.* And that left me a choice of admitting to something that never happened or being homeless on the street.

"You have a girlfriend. Her name is Kayla. Admit it," my mother said.

"But it's not true," I mustered.

"You have a girlfriend. Her name is Kayla. Admit it," my mother said.

"I don't though," I said.

"I won't be manipulated by you again. Make your decision. This isn't about me. *There's nothing wrong with Mommy.*"

I broke down, begging, pleading with my mother to believe me as the tears streamed down my face. My mother was unmoved.

"You have a girlfriend. Her name is Kayla. Admit it," my mother repeated, an edge in her voice.

I broke down, begging, pleading with my mother to believe me as the tears streamed down my face. My mother was unmoved. By now she had finished throwing my things into the garbage bag. She looked at me expectantly, her hands on her hips, her lips pursed, her emerald eyes blazing. I lived a lifetime in the ten seconds of silence that followed.

The little ember of myself that had been glowing with the fire of newfound hope smoldered and died.

"You're right. I'm sorry," I began.

"Say it," she said quietly, a smile playing at the edge of her lips.

"I have a girlfriend. Her name is Kayla. I admit it," I lied softly.

"Now you're going to tell your father and you're going to tell your sisters that you've been lying to them. And you're going to break everything off with this girl, and you are not to talk to her or her brother ever again. And if I find out you so much as say hi to them, you are out of my house. I have half a mind to throw you out anyway. Is that clear?"

I nodded, heartbroken, the tears still streaming down my cheeks. I was still sobbing ten minutes later when my mother dialed my father at work and I lied, telling him my mother's story about Kayla was true, my mother standing there holding the garbage bag full of my clothes in front of me as I did so.

"I had a feeling your mother was right," my father said on the phone. "The person you've been the last few weeks, laughing all the time, that just isn't you. I'm proud of you for admitting it. It's time to be a man." I thanked my father, told him I loved him through my tears.

I was still sobbing a half hour later when my sisters were brought into the kitchen for me to repeat the lie to them, my mother nodding approvingly.

And I was still sobbing that night when, alone in my bedroom, I opened my window, removed the screen, sat out on the ledge, and waited for the courage to jump. I sat there and prayed for a gust of wind to blow me off so I could die without having to do the act myself. But the wind didn't come and the courage never came and I sat there until dawn, tears streaming down my face, more ashamed than anything else. I did not have the courage to be the girl I was. I did not have the courage to stand up to my mother. I did not even have the courage to die.

I DID what my mother asked. I moved my seat in my classes, stayed away from David and Kayla, ignored their confused questions and apologies for whatever they did to hurt me and cause my absence. I went to class, kept to myself, came home and cried.

I was back to having no friends, and the widening gulf between me and the rest of the world constantly threatened to consume me. The dreams of the forest where I could still be me persisted, but they were taking a dark turn; now stormclouds filled the sky and instead of sunlight dancing between the leaves, it was rain. After a couple of weeks and three different nights of sitting on the ledge of my window, praying to G-d to give me the courage to jump, I sought out my mother and asked her to come to my bedroom to talk. I told her the truth, that I was actively suicidal, that I needed help, that I was going to kill myself unless I received that help, and I asked her, begged her, pleaded with her, to get me that help. Even after everything that had happened, after the preceding years of torture and pain, she was my mother. She would protect me from this, right? She would know what to do. She would know.

There was a long pause.

"How did you plan to do it?" she asked.

"Oh, I was going to jump off the windowsill," I said, showing her the loose screen.

My mother laughed, a rueful, humorless laugh.

"That won't kill you. Besides, even if somehow you did manage to die, your body would be bruised and your bones would be broken. Do you know how bad that would make me look?"

There was a sinking feeling in my gut as the world began to spin. My mother kept talking.

"It's so typically selfish of you. You can't even think of anyone but yourself even when you're fucking suicidal. You haven't even thought about what that would mean for me. I mean, if you really want to kill yourself, what you should do is hang yourself. You can have a kippah on at your funeral and we can hide the marks." My mother described, in detail, multiple ways she would dress me to do so and how happy she would be without me in her life.

"That is why you're going to do it, right? To make our lives better?"

I said nothing. The room was still spinning.

"I hope you do kill yourself. At least then I can be done with the biggest mistake of my life. You have caused me, your father, your sisters, nothing but pain. But this is so typical of you. You only told me this because you want your suicide to be about you. You won't even kill yourself for someone else. You're doing this for yourself."

She got up and walked towards the door.

"You're going to kill yourself for *attention*. What a joke. Well I won't give it to you. I won't play your game. If you actually care about me, you know what you have to do now."

She kissed the mezuzah on my bedroom door and left.

I cried for hours. I begged G-d to take me, to end it all. But somewhere in the darkness of that night, a tiny inner voice began to rise. To this day, I don't know where it came from. Maybe it was G-d telling me it wasn't my time. Maybe I needed to fully hit rock bottom before I could find my courage. Maybe it was coincidence, chance. Maybe it had always been there and I had just never noticed it. But it was a voice I'd never heard before, a voice that replaced tentativeness with conviction and despair with resolve. I could live, if only out of spite. I would live, if only because she *didn't* want me to. I was destined for better than whatever this was. I had to be. I would not waste myself, even if everyone around me saw me as a waste.

The next morning, my mother was surprised to see me.

I got all As in my second semester too.

TEN

At the end of my first semester of college, I had firmly decided I was going to law school. This was not because I wanted to be a lawyer. In point of fact, I did *not* want to be a lawyer at all. But after hearing my mother's stories about very nearly going to law school, I thought if I fulfilled her dream she would be proud of me – or at least live vicariously through me. In short, I thought I could buy my mother's love by living her dream. My mother, when I told her, frankly told me I was wasting my time because I wasn't smart enough to get in. But two semesters of straight As had taught me that I could handle the academics of college, and the pre-law advisors at McDaniel had no such qualms about my qualifications.

I may have been able to find the strength to stay alive, but my decision meant I wasn't going to be able to live that life for myself for a long time. I'd noticed my mother becoming weaker for some time; what had once been an iron grip was increasingly pliable, easily broken, though I dared not attempt to do so lest my father become involved. Around my seventeenth birthday she finally gave up on trying vinegar, mostly because at 5 foot 9, I was now too big for her to control. My mother was formally diagnosed with multiple sclerosis later that year, but the threats never stopped. Instead, she'd simply tell me that I was never too old for her to begin again and, mostly out of fear, I believed her. Or maybe by this point I was so conditioned that I never questioned it. In retrospect, the idea of a forty year old frail woman with multiple sclerosis having the physical strength to control a teenager who had gone through male puberty seems almost laughable. But such is the power of conversion therapy. You believe what you are told because you want to breathe, you want the pain to stop.

Living at home meant living not one, but multiple overlapping lies. I had to live the lie of being male. Now seventeen, puberty had done its work and I was years away from even learning about transitioning; I legitimately didn't even know that was possible. But I also had to inhabit the part my mother would have me play, or at least so long as I lived at home. That meant espousing her values, speaking her lines. Yet I thought I could simply bifurcate my reality and lie to her, as I had done with my first year papers. That plan failed spectacularly that fall, because when classes at McDaniel resumed, my sister Sabrina joined me.

Sabrina had been taking classes at Hood College in Frederick for years already. What had been evident a decade earlier – that she was a prodigious musical talent – had come to pass. In addition to her talents at the piano and vocally, she had been composing music of her own since she was thirteen or fourteen; my father had even set up a computer station in the basement for her to write music, complete with the latest composition software. She hadn't scored as high as I had on her SAT, but unlike me, she hadn't needed to. She'd been courted by multiple colleges eager to have a legitimate once-in-a-generation prodigy in their music programs, and thus she'd had her choice not just of schools, but of scholarships. Where I had applied out of desperation, she'd applied from legitimate choices.

Perhaps the competition my mother fostered between us still gave rise to a certain degree of enmity. Truthfully, I *was* jealous of her. She was creative, beautiful, graceful, brilliant, *a girl who had gone through female puberty,* everything I'd always wanted to be and wasn't. And I had expected – or perhaps hoped – that she would attend Hood instead. I'd wanted my own space, my own life, away from my parents and away from Sabrina's shadow, even if for only a few hours a day. It was not to be.

Ironically, I found out later that Sabrina, too, had felt trapped by this competition between us. She wrote me once that as much as I could never live up to who she was, she always felt like she was a failure for not winning a competition with a sibling who was, to our parents, a constant disappointment. She was the favorite. She was *supposed* to win. The pressure placed on her must have been immense. And yet here I was, the failure, the black sheep, the mistake who my mother openly wished she'd miscarried, and she could never seem to win outright. It wasn't fair to either of us, and Sabrina deserved her own limelight.

McDaniel was a small school – just 1600 undergraduates when I was there – but I soon found that our separate majors meant that Sabrina and I didn't have much in terms of overlap. We had a handful of acquaintances in common, but mostly she kept to the music department. Still, we did have a few classes in common. My mother made clear that I was not permitted to obtain a higher grade than Sabrina in any class where she and I were both enrolled, and – as I still had nowhere else to go – I was sure to keep my end of the bargain. Where Sabrina got an A on an assignment, I got an A-. Where she got an A-, I got a B+. I was sure to get just enough questions wrong on a test or quiz to give her the higher grade. And when I took a music class – McDaniel, as a liberal arts college, had that as a curriculum requirement regardless of major – I carefully calculated each assignment and missed just enough questions on the final to finish with a 90% for the class, ensuring that I would not get a higher grade than Sabrina did in any of her music classes. My mother was pleased, saying that doing this recognized that I didn't deserve the grades I was getting in other classes.

"You may be able to fool your professors into thinking you're not lazy and stupid," she told me after I threw the final in a comparative literature class with Sabrina so that she would get a higher grade than me. "But I know better. Sabrina has to work for every grade she gets. Somehow you can just read something and remember it. That's not being smart, it's just cheating." Sabrina got the highest grade in that literature class. I finished second.

None of this is to say that Sabrina needed the help, of course – and that was the sad irony. In demanding that I deliberately throw my grades, our mother was granting Sabrina unearned victories she didn't need and undermining the victories she was entirely capable of obtaining on her own. Somehow, too, she had entirely avoided the social atrophy I'd suffered from years of homeschooling, and thus she easily navigated friendships and relationships as naturally as she wrote symphonies on the piano. It didn't take long for her to develop a reputation as among the finest musical talents the college ever had, and her ethereal, graceful manner, entirely appropriate for an artist of her abilities, endeared her to everyone at McDaniel.

In some ways, Sabrina and I did bond during the three years we overlapped at McDaniel. By the end of my sophomore year, I was driving the two of us back and forth to class every day in our father's Bonneville. The daily drives gave us time together and we forged a very real bond and, more than that, a genuine friendship. We eventually decided together to tell our parents – who insisted we still call them "Mommy" and "Daddy," including publicly, even though we were both now in college – that we would be calling them "Mom" and "Dad" henceforth, and the look of incredulity on our mother's face when we informed them of this *together* was, in truth, a genuine delight. It is difficult to say that I miss much of my childhood. But I do miss the kinship I had with Sabrina in those days.

THERE WAS another benefit to Sabrina joining me at McDaniel: Our mother finally let me get a driver's license. Our mother had forbade it previously, not trusting that I wouldn't simply use the car to leave – which, in retrospect, wasn't far from the truth. Yet whilst she was perfectly happy to drive *me* to and from class every day, she wasn't about to embarrass Sabrina in that manner. And so, between my first and sophomore years, I went to driving school.

To be fair, I had been behind the wheel before. I'd driven both the small and large farm tractors around the fields, mowing and hauling. I'd logged more hours on that small tractor than anyone could count (but when my parents replaced it with a new John Deere, I was banned from driving *that*, to my consternation). I'd driven my father's F-150 around the front yard. But I'd never driven a car on an actual *road*.

What was supposed to happen in Maryland is that a new driver, after obtaining a learner's permit, drives a certain number of hours, logs them, and then takes their completed logbook and driving school certificate to the Department of Motor Vehicles (in Maryland, called the Motor Vehicle Administration or "MVA") and takes the driving test. However, my mother couldn't be bothered to actually drive with me to obtain those hours and my father was at work too often. The result was that my parents simply faked the entries in the logbook and told me I'd learn in driving school. The rather hilarious result was that I, after getting a perfect score on the written driving examination, spent the road test portion of the driving class crawling down the shoulder of the interstate at ten miles per hour, shrieking in fear, as the bewildered driving instructor looked at my logbook trying to understand how I didn't know what I was doing. Thankfully, after I explained the situation, she was kind enough to take me to a parking lot and give me some time to learn how to actually drive.

I still failed my road driving test the first two times I took it. My parents took this as a sign of my lack of intelligence.

"How do you fail a driving test?" my father asked after the second time.

"I should have known," my mother said simply.

The problem was parallel parking, which the driving instructor hadn't had time to show me and thus I didn't at all know how to do it when the test came. My two failed driving tests at the MVA had been the first and second times in my life parallel parking, and thus after the second failure, my father set up some construction barrels in the driveway and let me practice parallel parking in his Bonneville. I spent hours in that Bonneville practicing parallel parking that summer, and because I was comfortable in it, my father let me use the Bonneville to take the driving test for the third time. And I passed. Not wanting to break up what was obviously working, and since the Bonneville was now a decade old, my father said I could drive myself and Sabrina to class in it.

I loved that car. I loved the smooth hum of the six cylinders, the flat torque curve, the way its big boat of a body hated any kind of corners. But mostly, I loved the feeling of freedom it gave me. My mother had been right – if I'd had the opportunity before, I would have taken Bonnie and driven off into the sunset. I couldn't do that now – Sabrina would be in the car with me, and I knew if I just left her at McDaniel my absence would be noticed immediately – yet I still daydreamed of getting into Bonnie, getting onto I-70 westbound, and driving until the freeway ended, arriving somewhere in the western part of the country where no one knew who I was and my parents couldn't find me. My dreams changed, too; now, instead of being the little girl dancing in the forest, I was the teenage girl in her car, running away down the highway, outrunning the sorrow.

I STILL HAD my heart set on being valedictorian, however, but throwing classes to Sabrina meant I had to make up those GPA points elsewhere. I experimented with a handful of concentrations – economics, philosophy, psychology – but eventually settled on a dual major of political science and art history and a minor in economics. Political science was for law school. But art history was for me. My advisor, Dr. Susan Scott, was a brilliant professor always impeccably dressed with a brooch on her blazer, with kindly eyes and a keen mind, and with a love of Asian art that was as palpable as it was infectious. She taught her classes in the art history building, an ancient two story edifice with a single classroom on the main floor with heat that never worked and a gallery for students works on the second floor. I loved that building, loved the strange noises it made, and the slide projectors that Dr. Scott used when every other professor was using PowerPoint, and the way the floors made satisfying creaking noises when you stepped juuuust right on the cracks between the boards beneath the carpet.

I took every class Dr. Scott offered and loved every single one of them, mostly due to the enthusiasm she had for the material and the genuine zeal she had for explaining not just what each particular work was, but why and how it was crafted. After every class I would stay for hours, peppering her with questions about the artists and the contexts behind each work, and Dr. Scott was always kind enough to answer every single one. It wasn't until my junior year that she discovered I was colorblind, when I confused the silver pavilion and golden pavilion in Japan, unable to tell the difference between them. Dr. Scott wanted to take me on the department trip to Japan to see the art I was studying for myself, but my mother refused. She hadn't wanted me to go to college at all, and she certainly wasn't spending a dime more than was necessary on it. Even attending the annual trip to the Metropolitan Museum of Art in New York took hours of persuading before my mother would allow it.

If I'd had my druthers, I would have pursued an advanced degree in art history. Art history was just history from the perspective of cultures, rather than drab histories with names and dates. Learning art history meant not just understanding when events occurred and why, but how those events impacted the people who lived them. After all, what is art but an expression of the emotional states of people based on what's happening to them in their lives? And so I sought departmental honors in art history, and my senior thesis was 140 pages on Japanese Buddhist monochromatic ink painting, focusing on Sesshu Toyo. Dr. Scott and I remained close for years after I graduated – I called her "Aunt Sue" – but I never was able to tell her how much she meant to me during those years.

My political science advisor was Dr. Herb Smith, who was a bit of a legend in Maryland political circles. Unlike the old art history building, the political science department was in one of the newer structures on campus, clad entirely in brick and housing not just political science, but history, English, and economics classes as well. Dr. Smith's office was on the top floor, where he'd smoke in his office and answer my myriad questions, propping open his window to protect my "young lungs." Dr. Smith was less formal than Dr. Scott, wearing a sport jacket over a polo shirt and jeans. But he was no less dedicated to his students. He seemed uncertain what to make of me, perhaps more bemused by a sixteen year old in his class with an encyclopedic knowledge and no social skills whatsoever than anything else.

My parents disliked Dr. Scott because they found art history to be one of the liberal arts degrees that the conservative talk radio hosts they *still* listened to increasingly derided. Dr. Scott never knew this, and was taken with my father, in particular, from the first time they met, though she had her suspicions about my mother she never mentioned until later. But my parents *hated* the overtly liberal Dr. Smith, who my mother was convinced would discover – and then nurture – my secret.

What both Dr. Scott and Dr. Smith never knew was how much they enabled me to engage in small acts of rebellion against my parents, asserting myself as much as my circumstances would allow. As far as they knew, I was as conservative as the lines I recited indicated, even though most of them were reflex or muscle memory. Yet when my mother told me I must replace Dr. Smith as my political science advisor, I refused, lying that such changes weren't allowed. And when Dr. Scott chose me to present twice at the West Virginia University Art History Symposium, I told my parents my presentation was a class requirement even though it was no such thing; that allowed me to go. I ended up serving as a teaching assistant for both of them in my senior year, and it was gratifying seeing two people I truly admired trust me with real responsibility.

Still, I knew I had to avoid attracting too much attention to myself, especially with Sabrina on campus able to report back if I stepped too far out of line. Thus, for the most part, I did as I was told by my parents. When I joined the McDaniel chapter of the Maryland Student Legislature, I introduced the anti-abortion bill my mother wanted. When I answered a question in class, I parroted the lines she gave me at the beginning of each day. With Sabrina on campus, I didn't dare take unnecessary chances, because I didn't know how much would get back to our mother, and every slim act of defiance I ventured came with a high cost no one at McDaniel ever knew about. When I developed a crush on a girl in the comparative literature class Sabrina and I had together, Jamie, I begged Sabrina to keep it from our mother. She did – until Jamie sat with us at a poetry reading the three of us attended. My mother was furious, of course.

Yet what was confusing to me at the time was *why*. Having a crush on a girl was what I was supposed to be doing, right? Why was that a *bad* thing? My mother said it was because Jamie wasn't Jewish, but that just confused me more. Was it that she wasn't Jewish, or that she was out of my mother's control? Regardless, I did what my mother said and stayed away from Jamie after that.

A friend made a Facebook page for me my junior year, and my mother very nearly kicked me out of the house until I deleted it. My mother discovered that I had been handing in to her different homework than I was submitting to the professor – yes, I gave her fake assignments all four years of college – and she hired a separate conservative economics tutor to explain why trickle-down economics was factually correct and then sat there and watched whilst I wrote an essay about it.

Of course, in hindsight, I probably could have left home. If I had told a friend who lived on campus the truth about what my home life was actually like, if I had told Dr. Scott or Dr. Smith, if I had told *anyone*, maybe they could have done something. Maybe they would have let me stay with them. My mother was growing weaker by the day. Somewhere in the recesses of my mind, I could see that even then.

So why didn't I leave? Honestly, it was fear. It was denial. And it was shame.

By this point, it had been five years since she'd broken me in that first vinegarboarding session. I was like a trained dog, cowering instinctively when her owner raises his hand. Even when the owner is old and frail, even when the shock collar is gone and the whip is frayed, the dog still cowers and whimpers, the memory stronger than the torture ever was. To this day, I have nightmares about what my mother did to me. The house where I grew up will be haunted in my dreams until the day I die. The evidence of my eyes was that my mother could no longer control me, and yet I could not believe it, because the punishment if I was wrong was so dire.

I was ashamed of my own weakness. I was ashamed that I was so helpless, so completely controlled by a woman who could not control her own body, yet could force me to heel at the snap of a finger. I was ashamed that I could not assert myself. And there was a part of me that didn't actually believe my mother's weakness, that feared it was an act, that worried she may actually be omniscient and she would know whatever I did.

But mostly I was ashamed that I wanted to. Because the truly sick part of conversion therapy, the real mindfuck, is that it coerces you into battle with yourself. If I were to disclose what my parents were doing, had done, to me, I would have also had to disclose *why*. I would have had to tell them that I was still dreaming every night about being a girl. And then, I thought, they would conclude, like my mother had, that I was crazy. After all, my sisters didn't know what I was going through, and they *lived with me*. Why would anyone else believe me?

So I covered my shame and my self hatred in a thick coating of cockiness in class, slathered on like cream cheese clings to a bagel, and cried myself to sleep every night from what I saw in the mirror.

Still, there were small acts of rebellion. When I interned at the Maryland General Assembly, I let Dr. Smith place me with Sandy Rosenberg, a well known progressive legislator and early supporter of Barack Obama for president. My parents, who openly believed that Obama was a secret Muslim sent by communists in Kenya to destroy the United States, were furious. I told my parents that the placement was out of my hands, even though it very much was not; I simply wanted to see for myself whether progressive ideas were as dangerous as my parents claimed. It was less a white lie than it was a test of what I could get away with. Though I told no one at the time – lest it get back to my parents – my conclusion was that Rosenberg's positions and brand of politics made a lot more sense than anything my parents said.

ALSO THAT YEAR, I met Sarah. Sarah was also a political science major. She was girl-next-door pretty, and progressive, and smart, with short dark hair around neck length and fiery eyes. The first time I saw her, she was giving a speech in the student union on Constitution Day, and she was talking about civil rights in a way that stirred the same feelings in me that the Rabbi's sermons had done years before. I fell for her, *hard*; she was, after Danay, the first girl I ever truly loved. I hid about as well as you'd expect from a newly eighteen year old with no social skills to speak of, which is to say not at all.

Dr. Smith was the first to notice this.

"Ask her out," he said one day with a smile after noticing me being completely unable to speak around her.

Dr. Smith meant no harm, but his suggestion was impossible. Sarah was already in a relationship, but even if she wasn't, I was in no place to have a relationship of my own. We may have been similar in age, but I was years behind her – in maturity, in living, in knowing who I was. But there was another layer to that: As much as she represented the kind of person I was attracted to – smart, kind, pretty – she also was the kind of woman I wanted to be, and that complicated things even *more*. I watched her because I wanted to *be* her, because she was a lesson in the kind of woman I wanted to be one day. I still didn't know transitioning was possible, but that didn't stop me from taking notes just in case.

My parents figured out I was in love with Sarah the first time they saw me talk with her on campus, which only goes to show just how awkward I was. Still, I realized there wasn't a whole lot they could do about it. After all, Sarah didn't let anyone control *her*, and I wanted to be like *that*, so I simply told my parents what they wanted to hear and kept my head down at home. My mother tried various things to regain the control she recognized was slipping away, even sitting on campus and selecting a student she wanted me to ask out, and then writing a note she wanted me to give to that student, which in retrospect is just as creepy and weird as it sounds. I did what my mother asked, the girl thankfully turned me down, and I was greatly relieved.

Sabrina dated throughout college, had relationships had all the traditional firsts one would expect from college years. I didn't. I graduated college having never been on a date, having never kissed anyone, having never been intimate with anyone. In some ways, I had fallen even further behind my age group. In some ways, college was for me like high school is for most people. In other ways, it was simply me learning. I spent hours in the library reading everything I could get my hands on. I read Barack Obama's book, and that led me to Noam Chomsky, and Audre Lorde, and bell hooks, and Angela Davis, and Ta Nehisi Coates, and the Combahee River Collective. I read the New Testament and the Koran and Buddhist holy scrolls. I read Marx, and Lenin, and Mao. My mother would have thrown me out if I'd attended the Vagina Monologues, so I read the script in the library instead.

I didn't just read progressive and leftist writers. The more I read, the more I realized how little I knew, so I decided to just read everything I could get my hands on. Maybe my parents were right, so I read Ayaan Hirsi Ali and Glenn Beck and Bill O'Reilly; they were in the library, too. But in the progressive thinkers' writings, I found compassion, magnanimity, a desire to make the world better. In the conservatives' tomes, by contrast, I found only anger and grievance. It was the same anger and grievance which seemed to fuel my parents. My mother even described her multiple sclerosis in terms of grievance – she described it as a monster, and even compared its appearance to President Obama. Increasingly I found myself simply taking notes on how little conservatism seemed to care about people, instead being centered entirely on punishment and rage.

But I didn't just learn by reading. I would spend hours in the student union watching people interact with each other, taking notes on what they said to each other, how they said it, what body movements they made. I watched students flirt with each other, fight, talk. I took notes on their words and body language, then tried them out for myself in front of a mirror or in the shower. I paid special attention to Sarah, trying to mimic the sort of body language and statements she made. She seemed to have everything together, and that made her a guide for the person I wanted to be the day I finally figured everything out.

I was a long way from learning that you cannot become your

true self by copying other people. But I also had no foundation for who or what I was. The foundation I'd built before I came out, the headstrong little girl, had been too fragile, and crumbled under the weight of years of conversion therapy. That girl never did come back; she died in my teenage years. The foundation built in her place was stronger, more rigid, but also colder and formed out of the need to survive with bricks made out of observations and yearnings and tears.

ELEVEN

My senior year of college, my mother no longer doubted I would graduate. By now, her predictions that I'd be unable to cut it in college were proven wrong, and what had appeared to be a foolhardy prediction of being valedictorian suddenly seemed less so. My mother still believed I wouldn't make it into law school until I scored a 165 on my LSAT. At that point, my mother finally acknowledged reality, but she framed it rather differently than I expected.

"I always knew you could do it," she lied. "You just needed the motivation you got from me saying you couldn't."

My mother began talking about what she called the "hallowed halls" of law school, took me to see New York University and Pennsylvania University. It felt like she was, for the first time in my life and for a brief but glorious moment, truly proud of me. But for all of my academic achievements, my body wasn't keeping pace. My Crohn's Disease – which I still did not know I had, and would not be diagnosed with for another few years – flared badly during my senior year. I lost fifty pounds off of my already skinny 5 foot 9 inch frame, and was under a hundred pounds by graduation. When I finally persuaded my parents to take me to a doctor, I was relieved when my father offered to come with me and leave my mother at home. Trusting him, I let him come into the examination room with me. There was a knock at the door, and the doctor entered.

"Stuart's fine," my father told the doctor before I could say anything. "He just exaggerates a lot. He's feeling a lot better."

The doctor left without examining me.

I was not, in fact, fine, throwing up every night and unable to keep more than a couple of meals down. Yet when graduation came, I was co-valedictorian, with a 4.12 GPA. After it was announced and the graduation ceremony was over, I came bounding off the stage. *Now* my mother would be proud of me, I thought. *Now* she would believe in me. I gave Sabrina a hug, said "your turn next year!" and turned to my parents.

My mother was furious.

"How dare you humiliate Sabrina like that!" she screamed at me.

I was legitimately confused. *I had just been valedictorian, just like I promised.* But my mother believed that I had been valedictorian just to show up Sabrina, that I had only managed it by doing an "easy program like art history." To my mother, if Sabrina failed to be valedictorian next year, people would wrongly believe I was smarter than she was. All the classes I had thrown so Sabrina would get better grades in them meant nothing to my mother because by being valedictorian, she said I had broken my word.

My mother later said that me being valedictorian was one of the worst days of her life, because it made her pride and joy look bad and aggrandized myself. She viewed it as selfish and arrogant, quintessentially me. Worse was that as I had crossed the stage to receive the award, the professor had announced my departmental honors in art history and my hope to one day get an advanced degree in the discipline – something my mother saw as embracing my queerness and thus a betrayal. It didn't matter that I was locked into law school at this point, having accepted a scholarship offer at the Catholic University of America's Columbus School of Law the fall before; as far as my mother was concerned, I had publicly humiliated her. Law school would still be my ticket out, but knowing that the most fundamental reason I had for going, to make my mother proud of me, was off the table had me feeling increasingly as though I had made a terrible mistake.

WITH BOTH SABRINA and me in college, only Elaina was left at home. She had grown a lot since the little girl who scrawled "r-a-r-e" on everything she saw, thinking it was her name. Still, though, she was much younger than either of us, so she was barely a teenager when Sabrina joined me at McDaniel. Both Sabrina and I were fiercely protective of Elaina; each of us had a pet name for her, and though we differed greatly in our childhood experiences, we both recognized that it was best to protect Elaina as best we could from what we both saw as our mother's unpredictability. Thus, after starting college, though I never told Sabrina all – or even most – of what our mother did to me, Sabrina knew enough about our mother's temper to agree that Elaina needed to be shielded from it.

Elaina had grown up rather differently than Sabrina or I. Elaina was beautiful, a spitting image of our grandmother, quick witted, always ready with a perfectly times joke or punch line. Sabrina, like I had before her, had scored exceptionally well on standardized testing. Elaina's gifts lay elsewhere, but were no less impressive. From an early age she was gifted with the written word; she won an award in a local competition for a Star Wars story she wrote before she was seven. As a teenager, she wrote for the *Carroll County Times,* interviewing Major League Baseball players like Curtis Granderson and Nick Markakis and broadcasting trailblazers like Suzyn Waldman; all were entranced by Elaina's easy facility with storytelling.

Elaina had a true talent with words that needed to be

nurtured, but my mother didn't understand what a gift Elaina had. Instead, when Sabrina and I would come home from McDaniel, our mother would complain to me that she wished Elaina had my test scores and vice versa. Frankly, Elaina didn't need them; she was just as smart as I had been at her age, if not more so. Our mother simply couldn't see it. Our mother understood only those gifts which benefited *her*, and she simply couldn't brag about a gifted writer the way she could about a ninety-ninth percentile test score.

My mother's penchant for seeing her children as tools she could use for self advancement, combined with her increasing baseless disappointment with Elaina, led to what came next. Our mother had joined an online homeschooling group led by yet another evangelical Christian conservative with far-right views. As she had done so often in the past, our mother, wanted to ingratiate herself to her new friend. This leader had a teenage son, Joshua, about Elaina's age, who had terminal pediatric cancer. Joshua's mother knew he was lonely and wanted to introduce him to Elaina. That wouldn't have been objectionable by itself, but despite knowing both the diagnosis and prognosis, the two of them agreed for some time to *not tell Elaina about it.* They even told Joshua not to say anything to Elaina either. Our mother encouraged Elaina to date Joshua, meaning that Elaina's first ever boyfriend was dying of cancer and for weeks Elaina did not know.

Elaina eventually found out – Joshua told her the truth not long before he died – and Elaina was justifiably devastated by the news. Sabrina and I did everything we could to keep Elaina hopeful, but none of us knew how precarious Joshua's prognosis really was. Meanwhile, both Sabrina and I were furious with our mother and confronted her one weekend, telling her flatly that she had set up Elaina for an unbearable trauma and this was unacceptable. She needed to come clean to Elaina, we both thought. Our mother simply said it was not our place to judge her; besides, she said, by providing Elaina to comfort a dying child, she'd done a good deed.

But Elaina was barely 14, not remotely ready for a loss like this. When it came, she was entirely blindsided, and our mother compounded her pain by providing no therapist or assistance in processing the biggest loss of her life. Within weeks, Elaina had what can only be described as a nervous breakdown. She began seeing Joshua, seeing our dead grandfather, seeing dead animals walk around the house and the farm, running after and speaking with specters and ghosts only visible to her. Sabrina and I begged our mother to get Elaina the help she needed, but our mother said simply that there was no evidence Elaina needed help. After all, our mother said, perhaps she really *was* seeing the ghosts or spirits of our grandfather or Joshua. It got to the point where our mother started openly speculating that maybe Elaina was seeing these specters because she was the Jewish messiah, and therefore she would be forever remembered as the messiah's mother.

Our mother became head of the homeschooling group, though, recommended by Joshua's mother, so she got what she wanted. Her glee at this result caused an epiphany for me. It was at this point that I started realizing what my mother truly was – not an omniscient god with a fierce temper casting judgment upon my sin, but a sad and pathetic woman motivated entirely by being liked. She wasn't homophobic and transphobic because she thought being queer was a sin. She was homophobic and transphobic because she didn't want people to know her as the mother of a queer child.

Elaina was barely recovering, by herself, without help, when our grandmother passed away towards the end of my college years. She had left my father and each of her three grandchildren a sizable inheritance – between her house and the building in Scarsdale that formerly held my grandfather's pharmacy, her estate was worth well over a million dollars – and my father's plan was to use his money to retire and ours to pay for our educations through any graduate school we wanted to attend. My mother, however, had different plans. There was no point in my father retiring, she said, as the three of us were all grown up. Thus she pushed my father to go back to work, which he eventually did, taking a job producing videos with the Department of Health and Human Services.

Our mother viewed the lack of a gift from my grandmother to her as a personal affront, and in addition to taking the money that our father had wanted to use for retirement, decided to take my share as well. She used much of the money to extensively remodel the house. Gone was the old farmhouse kitchen with old wooden cabinets and white wallpaper covered in sheaves of wheat. In its place was an open concept modern kitchen with stainless steel appliances and an island and real granite countertops and a gas stove. And with my portion, she bought herself a new car — a Saturn Outlook, of all things, with every option, that cost over fifty thousand dollars. I hadn't earned an inheritance from my grandmother, she told me, but she *had*. Still, she said there was money left that she would give me to help with paying off law school loans when I graduated.

A year later, Elaina was preparing to go to college. My mother's massive spending had meant Elaina had needed to land a large scholarship to afford a private school, and that wasn't to be. The public college that my parents had told Elaina they'd allow her to attend was going through a very public crisis of sexual assaults, and I feared for her safety there. I asked my mother to give my law school money to Elaina, so she could go to a college truly of her choice. My mother need not tell Elaina where the money came from, I said, just tell Elaina it was a gift from them. My mother looked at me confused for a moment, then smiled thinly and laughed heartily. The money never existed, my mother said. She'd lied to me, hoping that the promise of money would compel me to finish law school. She'd spent all of my inheritance on her kitchen and her car.

THUS, by this time, my relationship with my parents was quickly deteriorating. When law school started that fall, I moved into a first floor garden apartment in Hyattsville. The walls were thin – I could hear every argument and every bit of makeup sex my upstairs neighbors had, both of which were daily occurrences. It was infested with roaches. The unit below me was a party space which meant that twice a week there would be a wedding, loud music would play late into the night, and I wouldn't get any sleep. But it was *mine*.

Thanks to Dr. Smith, I landed a job as a campaign manager for a moderate Republican county board candidate in central Maryland. Living in Hyattsville meant I would drive two hours one way to work after classes, and then two hours back, but I didn't care. My first paycheck was just enough to buy the Bonneville from my parents for a thousand dollars. It was in pretty terrible shape by this point, with over 300,000 miles, a shifter than only sometimes worked, a sagging headliner, and a key that wouldn't come out of the ignition, none of which I had the money to fix. The car was in such poor condition that when I woke up one morning to find it had been stolen (it was, alas, that kind of neighborhood), the thieves actually brought it back that afternoon, minus a few interior pieces and a full tank of gasoline. Still, Bonnie continued to run and drive and do all I asked of her.

The pay at my job was terrible – just enough for my rent and three bags of potatoes every month. Like many queer kids, even closeted ones, moving out meant getting cut off from financial help from your parents; my mother made clear there would be no financial assistance for me regardless of what happened. This point was punctuated when she turned off my cell phone on Yom Kippur; I truly was on my own.

Yet in a strange way, my mother's treatment of me had prepared me for what was to come. The Shoppers Food Ware-house a half mile from my apartment was within walking distance, so I would go there, buy a couple of bags of potatoes, and then have three potatoes a day for my meals – one each for breakfast, lunch, and dinner. Sometimes, when I was really lucky, the Shoppers would have slices of old cake for $1 each, the remnants of bakery items a few days before, and I would buy a couple and bring them home as a treat. I was often late on rent, and came home to demands from the landlord or even eviction notices on my door, but the threats from my mother taught me not to overreact, and I would eventually get the money together to pay. Strangely, I found it was easier to explain matters to the landlord than to my mother; the landlord, at least wouldn't call me a lazy abomination.

Having my own place and my own car meant a degree of freedom I'd never had before. For the first time, I began wearing women's underwear, because my mother could not stop me. I wasn't even sure why at this point – the idea of transitioning was still years away, but it just *felt right*. I saw the word "transgender" in an article in law school and began researching it, wondering if this actually described what I was. Unable to afford car maintenance, I traded LSAT lessons to the friendly young man at the local independent mechanic's shop for oil changes and brake jobs.

Law school was a blessing. Yes, I attracted some attention for being the youngest student in my class by more than a couple of years, with some students calling me a "gunner" for my young age and penchant for asking questions after class. Still, my grades, whilst good, weren't extraordinary, and I was just fine with that. I didn't actually want a whole lot of attention on myself, and I really just wanted to get by as best I could.

At first, not wanting to abandon my sisters, I'd drive home and spend the night on Friday, go to Shabbos services with my family on Saturday morning, and then drive home. Then, one day, Sabrina pulled me aside and confided in me that after I'd moved out, our father had started hitting Elaina. Sabrina told me that Elaina had showed her the bruises. I took my sisters for a drive, asked Elaina if this was true, and she confirmed it. And then Elaina begged me to take her with me, to let her live with me in my apartment.

My first thought was to tell her yes. That night I spent searching on the internet how to gain custody over your younger sibling. I was a law student, I thought, in a school filled with lawyers, surely this had to be doable. But then I emailed a couple of professors, read their responses cautioning me about how this would be a lot harder than I thought, and I hesitated. I was 20. I had just started law school. I was flat broke. Bringing my 15 year old sister to live with me meant a custody fight with my parents, and that was a fight I frankly was in no position to start, to say nothing of winning. My mother had just sued two different general contractors for not completing her kitchen to her desired specifications, and won both times, and she now had my father's inheritance to fall back on for resources. Meanwhile, I would have to drop out of law school, get a second job, and do the case *pro se*, at the very least.

Sabrina was adamant she was going to graduate school for music out of state, so Elaina going with her wasn't an option. I had a choice: I could choose Elaina or choose myself. And to my 20 year old self it felt categorically unfair that once again, Sabrina gets everything she wanted, whilst once again I was stuck.

I should have prioritized Elaina. I should have said damn the practicality, damn the money, get in the car, we'll figure it out. But I was scared. I was scared of what my parents would do. I was scared of the police coming to my door because I knew my parents would call them. I was scared of leaving law school, which felt like my one shot at a ticket out of that place. I was scared of losing the tenuous hold I had on my true self, now that I finally had the opportunity to explore it. I was scared of losing the freedom I had for the first time in my life.

I chose myself.

I told myself I couldn't challenge my parents for custody, that doing so was foolhardy, that I could not drop out of law school after everything I'd sacrificed to get there. And they sounded like very good reasons in my head. But truthfully, I was afraid. After everything they'd done, I turned out to be still be the scared child sitting there limply as I was waterboarded with vinegar, complying because I feared the alternative. And *that* thought made me so disgusted with myself that I did something which I can only describe as colossally stupid.

I mustered my courage, tried to appear as menacing as possible, and the next morning confronted my parents in my mother's newly remodeled kitchen in front of Sabrina and Elaina. Even worse, I flatly told them I didn't believe their denials and *instructed* them to stop hitting Elaina. All I'd done, of course, was let them know that Elaina had told me they were hitting her, thereby eliminating her ability to do so in the future. But I returned to my apartment thinking I'd saved the day, that I had scared them into compliance without sacrificing my fragile life.

It was a very good self deception.

By my next visit the following weekend, Elaina had recanted the entire story, saying through tears at the kitchen table that I'd invented the entire affair for my own purposes. And there was a familiar mechanical, robotic timbre to the words that I recognized only too well because they were the words of someone who had been programmed, broken. My mother had done the same thing to me enough times for me to know *exactly* what happened during that week in my absence. I had sounded exactly the same way when I said something required by my mother after a session of vinegar.

I had assumed that my mother wouldn't do that kind of thing to Elaina. I had guessed, even after Joshua, even after the hitting, that the extreme abuse I'd suffered for years was unique to me, that my mother had a unique hatred for me that she would not spread or take out on her other children. I had thought that Elaina, who wasn't queer, wasn't willful, never misbehaved, had nothing but goodness in her heart, would be protected from the worst of my parents' excesses. And I had guessed horribly, catastrophically, and worst of all, *predictably* wrong. My threats and bluster had been a bluff that my mother had called without a second thought. And so, as Elaina, in tears in front of our parents, denied anything ever happened, my heart shattered into pieces that never fully healed.

Elaina was furious with me for betraying her. I didn't blame her. She didn't want to come live with me any more, and I didn't blame her for that either. She never forgave me.

I never forgave myself either.

TWELVE

The best day of my first semester of law school was when Sarah came to see Catholic University, as she was also considering law school. I still carried a torch for her, but still wasn't going to do anything about it (though I did get a dozen donuts for her just so she would be able to pick the flavor she wanted). But that visit did get me thinking about how far behind I was socially. Sabrina and Elaina were both in relationships by this point, and I still hadn't ever been on a date, let alone kissed anyone. So I made a Facebook page and, still having never been on a date, let alone kissed anyone, made a profile on the Jewish dating website JDate. After a couple of conversations that went nowhere, I connected with Ashley.

Ashley was the same age as me, slim, pretty, spray tanned, with a small star tattoo on her left wrist, a nose ring, and a quick temper. I had never dated anyone before, so the fact that she was interested in me at all was as confounding to me as it was tantalizing. She was from Chicago's North Shore, where her father was one of the best consumer attorneys in the country; she herself was a rising senior at Illinois State University. After a couple of weeks of online talking, we decided to meet in person, and she caught a flight to Reagan Airport. We agreed she'd stay at a hotel the first time out, but I still showed her around the city and took her out to dinner. Things progressed quickly from there, and after a couple of months we were dating exclusively. I hadn't told Ashley about my transness yet; that would come much later.

My parents wanted to meet my very first girlfriend, so I took her to the farm one Friday night to meet them during my customary Shabbos trip to check on my sisters. I wasn't expecting it would be the *last* time I would see my parents in person.

Things had begun badly. My mother was incensed when she saw Ashley.

"Why do you have a beautiful girlfriend?" she asked me angrily, evidently not at all comprehending the contrast between her emotions and the words.

"Most parents would be happy for their kids if that happened to them," I responded evenly. Law school had sharpened my wits a bit, and living by myself had made me more daring. My father was more circumspect; he knew what came next, because my mother was not going to permit me to have a relationship outside of her control. On the surface, having a girlfriend was exactly what my mother always wanted for me. Yet Ashley was *very* liberal, outspokenly in favor of queer rights and marriage equality, explicitly antizionist, all of which was unacceptable to my mother, who suddenly, in a strange bit of affirmation, considered the relationship (not incorrectly) lesbian and therefore an abomination. What my mother wanted was a relationship with traditional gender roles, and even if it appeared outwardly cisheteronormative, this was most assuredly not that.

My mother and sisters (undoubtedly at my mother's urging) spent dinner cruelly mocking Ashley's appearance until she cried. I was furious, demanded an apology in vain. Talking with my mother in the laundry room was like talking with a brick wall; our conversation deteriorated rapidly until my mother, citing a list of all of the ways I had let her down, predicted I would soon become an organ donor. I archly responded that I already was.

In some Jewish communities, being an organ donor was prohibited because of the Jewish law requiring a person be buried whole. Still, I considered that being an organ donor was an example of the principle of Pikuach Nefesh, the Jewish ideal that there is nothing more important than saving a human life, even if doing so requires violating another commandment.

My mother was not remotely persuaded by my argument and asked Ashley and me to leave first thing in the morning without accompanying them to services. As I turned to depart the laundry room, she called after me.

"Stuart," she said. "Never tell anyone what you are. Never tell Ashley. Never tell anyone."

On my way to the guest room – for my parents insisted that Ashley and I sleep in separate bedrooms, so she took my old bedroom whilst I took the guest room – I stopped to say good night to my father.

"No matter what," I told him. "Promise me we'll always talk. Promise me those fathers and children we see in the movies who don't talk will never be us." My father didn't respond. He just gave me a bear hug, tighter than I'd ever felt from him, and I went to bed. Ashley, meanwhile, poked in an hour later, deciding we should get back at my mother by having sex on their couch whilst my parents were asleep.

A COUPLE OF MONTHS LATER, I came home from work feeling woozy.

It was during the summer between my first and second years of law school. I was still throwing up on a daily basis, but I still didn't know exactly what was going on because I couldn't afford a doctor and didn't have health insurance. The kindly old doctor at the clinic at Catholic University had run some bloodwork and was able to determine I had some kind of autoimmune condition along with a myriad of vitamin deficiencies, but couldn't narrow it down more than that without tests there was no way I would be able to afford. In the meantime, I alternated between his prescriptions of promethazine and metoclopramide, which helped with the nausea but did nothing for the weird radiating pain in the right lower quadrant of my abdomen that was, by now, a constant companion.

Thus my wooziness wasn't necessarily unexpected when I arrived at my apartment, but it was unusually strong on this day. I thought it was maybe due to the unusual heat and humidity, but the air conditioning in my apartment didn't help. I sat down on my bed, waiting for the wooziness to pass, felt a strange sensation in my left arm. I looked down, saw it shaking uncontrollably, but it didn't *feel* like it was shaking.

"That's weird," I tried to say, but nothing came out. And then my knees gave way and I collapsed onto the carpeted floor, drooling and shaking uncontrollably. I remember ordering my legs to stand, my arms to prop me up, but all four of my limbs stubbornly refused. I lived a decade in the minutes I spent on the floor, as thoughts and images came and went. I chided myself for not vacuuming the carpet. I imagined I saw rescuers coming to get me, only to realize my eyes were closed and I was seeing nothing at all, only to realize my eyes were not closed at all, they were just fixed and unblinking, and yet I could not see.

I was lucky. Ashley was visiting that week and had been in the shower when I passed out; she came out of the shower, saw me, and called 911. I came out of my stupor, saw her, asked what was going on, then collapsed again, my left arm contorting at an unnatural angle as I started shaking again and my mind went blank.

I'd had two full grand mal seizures by the time I arrived at the hospital by ambulance. Neurological tests showed my brain lighting up like the proverbial Christmas tree, but the neurologist was puzzled because the readings came and went; they showed none of the damage that seizures should be showing, yet showed the same symptoms and patterns when active. Weirder still was the CT scan of my abdomen that showed massive levels of nondescript inflammation; doctors weren't sure if they were connected, but they were certain something was wrong. Ashley wasn't legally able to consent to treatment as my girlfriend, and I was in no position to decide anything for myself. By my second day in the hospital, my left hand was twisted into a strange clawlike visage even when I wasn't seizing. So the doctors at the hospital called my parents.

My mother at first believed I was faking it, interrogating Ashley and saying that I couldn't have had a seizure because Ashley had never seen a seizure before and thus had no frame of reference. When the doctors confirmed I had, in fact, had multiple seizures, my mother called her health insurance to confirm I was no longer on their policy; she knew the stay would be expensive and didn't want to be billed. She then told the doctors to discharge me. The doctors warned against it, recommending that the inflammation in my GI tract be biopsied and that I have a sleep study and MRI of my brain.

If my mother had consented to those tests, the doctors would have learned that the inflammation in my abdomen was from moderate to severe Crohn's Disease, that as a result of the swelling and tissue death in my intestine from the Crohn's I was severely malnourished, that the Crohn's had caused my constant vomiting and nausea from repeated bowel obstructions, and that it was severe vitamin deficiencies that had caused my seizures. I would have been placed on immunomodulators for the Crohn's and vitamin shots, and could have made a full recovery.

My mother did not consent to those tests. Instead, my left arm still contorted into a claw, unable to see out of my right eye, I was discharged. My mother told me that my secret gayness – still, only my parents knew who and what I truly was – was causing me stress that was killing me, gave me the contact information for a program that "helped" people like me. It was basically conversion therapy for adults.

"Stress kills, and sins are stress," she told me as I wobbled unsteadily to the car. It was the last time I ever saw her.

A couple of days later, my hand had unclenched. My vision had not returned and would not return for months; it was the second semester of my 2L year before I could see anything out of my right eye again. Finally able to speak, I called my father, told him that I was really sick, that I needed help. And after twenty years of holding everything in – the vinegar, the beatings, the work, the mind games – I recited what my childhood had been, naming one nightmare after another. I asked him how he could allow this, why he would play her games, why he would subject *Elaina* to what had been done to me, why he could say he loved me after helping my mother waterboard me.

And I begged him for help.

There was a long pause on the phone, the longest pause I'd ever heard in my life, a pause so long I was worried time was distorting and I was going to seize again.

Then my father's voice came back.

"I know," he said. "Everything you're saying is true." Another pause. His voice grew softer, as though he was choking back tears. "There's nothing I can do."

He hung up the phone. I called him back. It went to voicemail.

I never spoke with my father again.

ESTRANGEMENT IS A STRANGE FEELING, like being an orphan when your parents are still alive. My mother left a voicemail on my phone a month later, letting me know they were sitting shiva for me, that I was dead to them, that she was mourning me, that she was very sad for my loss. In a way, I envied her. She buried the son she never had, and in so doing was able to get a degree of finality I never attained.

It would be a lie to say that my entire childhood was nothing but horrors. I do have good memories, from playing baseball in the backyard with my father to my mother looking at me approvingly when I was accepted to law school. But those good memories make the painful ones all the more potent, because I know my parents were capable of love, capable of loving *me*, and yet simply did not. And to my shame, I tried to buy that love anyway.

I spent the first twenty years of my life pursuing the approval of parents who were never going to grant it, no matter what I did. In pursuing that approval, I did things I am not proud of. I abandoned my sister, choosing my future and safety over hers. I unquestioningly accepted my mother's view of Zionism, participated in virulently racist pro-Israel rallies, claimed not to be white on college and law school applications because of my Jewish identity. I told my sisters I would hit them, punch them, because my mother ordered me to as part of her endless attempts to drive a wedge between us and I was afraid of being waterboarded again. I walked into a woman's dressing room when she wasn't clothed, without knocking. I espoused racist and anti-choice precepts in college classes, fearful she would know if I didn't.

Individually, these would be unforgivable. Together, they are damning.

It would be easy to say I wasn't in control of my actions. True, my mother had thoroughly broken me. A person, a *child*, can only take so much torture before they accede to any demand, no matter how grievous, just to prevent it from happening again. Yet that is cold comfort to the people hurt, who saw not a terrified little girl, but a cocky teenaged white person leveraging their white privilege to do harm. And it's also not entirely true, for whilst I may have been conditioned, may have been coerced, I still had a choice. I could have refused. I could have chosen more waterboarding, more vinegar, more torture. Yes I was a child. I still had a mind of my own. I chose to do harm. I have always believed impact is more important than intent, and my intent – to save myself from further pain – was, in the final examination, selfish. I was too absorbed with avoiding my own discomfort to reckon with the consequences of my actions.

Thus, my estrangement from my parents brought both relief and no relief at all. Estrangement gave me true freedom to question everything I'd been taught, everything I'd assumed was true. It also taught me the cost of what I'd done. I now carried the burden not just of my childhood, not just of what my childhood had cost me, but what my childhood had cost others, too.

The truly fucked up part of conversion therapy is that it creates broken people, and broken people break other people. It was this realization which broke me the night I received my mother's message that she had sat shiva for me. What broke me was not that I had lost my parents, for it was easy to recognize I'd never really had them. I'd never been the son they wanted, and never would be. No, what caused me to cry into my pillow at night for years thereafter was that I had spent my first two decades chasing the approval of my parents *when I was never going to obtain it*. It was bad enough that I had harmed other people, but harming other people *for no reason* was more than I could stand.

And worse, I blamed myself for all of it, because I believed that I had brought it all on myself by being a girl in the first place. I had developed shame around my queerness because it had brought me nothing but pain, because it had caused my parents to torture me, because my parents' torture had led me to hurt other people, and I had sought their approval for nothing. Before, I had cried myself to sleep wanting to be a girl. Now I cried myself to sleep because I didn't deserve to be one, because the whole thing was just so pointless.

It was this which caused me used me to grow a goatee and later a beard, when doing so worsened my dysphoria. I wanted to *punish* myself. I wanted to feel dysphoria. I wanted the terrible feelings. But in the depths of my depression, I realized that law school was a gift as well as a privilege. For everything I had done, I was still a white middle class kid who'd gotten into law school at 20 and managed to get into law school.

And a law degree gave me a path to something that I now wanted more than anything in the world: Redemption.

THIRTEEN

My estrangement from my parents, and the complete lack of relationship with extended family, meant that I really no longer had any reason to remain in Maryland. Not having anywhere else to go and completely broke, I accepted Ashley's offer to move in with her. I transferred to Loyola University in Chicago for my last year of law school, packed my few belongings into boxes and mailed them to myself, and hopped on a plane for Chicago. I sold the Bonneville for $375 to someone who wanted the tires, cried when she was hoisted onto the tow dolly. I'd wanted to drive Bonnie there instead, but Ashley insisted there was no chance she'd have made the 1200 mile trip. In hindsight, she probably wasn't wrong.

When I arrived at the airport, Ashley was nowhere to be found. I called and texted her, and received no answer. This wasn't exactly the warm welcome I expected, and my fears only grew when Ashley, four hours later, curtly told me to take a cab and meet her at her mother's house. She was in a bad mood; I'd learned to recognize those, but I had yet to learn just *how* bad those moods could be. When I arrived, Ashley was angry about something or other, and in a fit of pique, grabbed my left wrist. I thought she was going to hug me and was completely unprepared for when she bent it backwards as hard as she could, not stopping until the cracking sound from my wrist was joined by my own screams in pain.

Ashley was profusely apologetic the rest of the night. She told me it was an accident, that she'd never intended to hurt me, that sometimes she lost control of her temper and it would never happen again. To prove it, she introduced me to her father and asked him to hire me for my final year of law school. I should have listened to the little voice in the back of my mind warning me, telling me that this would *not* be the last time, that this was going to be a disaster.

I didn't. I had nowhere else to go. I didn't even have a car to sleep in. I was completely in her control, and she knew it. So I accepted her father's job offer, accepted her apologies, and told myself I was overreacting, that she was in earnest when she meant it. And when a few months later she threw a shoe at my head, then apologized and once again swore it would never happen again, I told myself the same things. It was an isolated incident, I told myself. It had only happened twice. And besides, I told myself, I deserved it for the things I'd done. It was that last factor which led me to disregard the warnings of my college friend MaTt, who told me flatly to end the relationship because abuse did not stop once started. After all, if I deserved it, I had no one to blame but myself.

Ashley was right that she'd eventually stop – but what stopped was the apologies, not the hitting. By the time we got married my 3L year, she was hitting me on a weekly basis. Depending on the day, she'd punch me with a closed fist, slap me, shove me into a wall, elbow me, grab my head and squeeze as hard as she could, bend my wrists back. I never, ever fought back. After all, I reasoned, I deserved it.

Finally attending law school for myself instead of my parents, I excelled in my final year of law school, posting my best grades – ones comparable to what I'd received in college. Still, combined with my grades my first two years, it was only good enough for the top third of my class. Dr. Scott came to my graduation, was surprised I didn't rank higher and wanted to know what happened. I didn't care; just graduating was an accomplishment.

And so, after I graduated law school, I began preparing for the bar exam. The night before I was to take the exam, I was doing some last minute studying and eating carrot sticks with ranch dressing, part of a concerted effort I was making to eat healthier my 3L year in hopes of curing whatever it was that ailed me. It was an effort that would turn out badly. Around 9:00 pm, I started feeling a crushing pain in my stomach and my abdomen began to swell. The nausea and vomiting came shortly thereafter, and within an hour, I was in severe distress as my eyes began to yellow.

Living in Chicago with a job meant I had insurance for the first time, and therefore a doctor. Working full time and going to law school full time had meant we hadn't had much room in my schedule for medical tests to figure out what was wrong with me, but I had given him the full rundown of my symptoms over the past decade, and blood tests had once again confirmed *something* autoimmune. Thus, when I called the doctor that night and asked him for something for my stomach flu, something clicked in his mind as he finally understood what it was that I had, what had caused my symptoms and my seizures, why the nausea and vomiting were cyclical.

"This is not the stomach flu. You have a bowel obstruction, probably from Crohn's Disease or ulcerative colitis," he said. "You need to go to the emergency room *now*." I objected I had the bar exam the next morning, but the doctor was not to be questioned.

"Get off the phone with me and get to the emergency room. I'm not joking."

So I went. By the time I arrived, the button on my jeans had literally been broken off from my ever-expanding gut, and the pain was so severe I was almost in tears. Between dry heaves and bouts of vomiting, I managed to tell the very understanding doctor –in her very first month of residency, no less – that I needed to get back home for the bar exam the next morning. Yet she already knew that wouldn't be happening. A CT scan confirmed my doctor's suspicions of a bowel obstruction, and a later biopsy confirmed my Crohn's Disease.

Crohn's Disease is a type of autoimmune disease, a set of illnesses where the body's immune system cannot differentiate between invaders and the body's own tissues. In Crohn's, the immune system begins attacking the intestine, causing inflammation and scar tissue. This scar tissue can resemble a road, which gave the signature look of Crohn's-addled intestine its name: cobblestoning. Because Crohn's is progressive, over time the inflammation spreads and worsens, causing nausea and vomiting as the intestine loses the ability to digest and move food matter. Sometimes, it can even swell shut, or a bit of fibrous food matter can become stuck on a protrusion of scar tissue, causing a complete intestinal blockage. Untreated, the blockage can be deadly, as the intestine swells and leaks, causing sepsis. Crohn's is famously susceptible to stress, but unlike irritable bowel syndrome, the damage caused by Crohn's flares is permanent and incurable. One of the reasons the vinegar had stung so badly was the fumes and acidic liquid were touching open wounds on their way through my digestive tract, like pouring lemon juice in a thousand paper cuts – inside my body.

My Crohn's had been untreated for over a decade by this point, which caused massive damage to my terminal ileum, the part of my intestine that absorbs nutrients. That had caused vitamin deficiencies that in turn caused my seizures a couple of years before. My intestine had scarred over, which had caused the bouts of nausea and vomiting when I would eat something my body couldn't digest. And I had spent the night before the bar exam eating fibrous carrot sticks, the final blow to my besieged intestine; a bit of carrot had gotten stuck, then triggered a sudden flare. My intestine had swollen shut so completely even liquids could not pass through.

There would be no attending the bar exam the next morning. The doctor told me frankly that if I left to go to the bar exam, I would be dead before the first day of the test was over. There were only two options: emergency surgery to remove the blockage, or the insertion of a nasogastric tube. The tube was faster, and time was of the essence, so the doctor opted for that. Whilst I was still awake and without any numbing, the doctor and her team inserted a large tube down into my stomach through my nose and throat to suck out any matter still in my intestine and then forcibly reopen the part that had swollen shut. The tube had to remain there for most of my weeklong hospital stay.

The Crohn's Diagnosis would change my life. I was now on a restricted diet – no nuts, no seeds, no raw fruits or vegetables, nothing with more than three grams of dietary fiber per serving, no deli meats, no non-ground animal proteins, and strict limits on my fat, salt, and sugar intakes. Even still, the first gastroenterologist I saw after I was discharged from the hospital gave me a life expectancy of 55 to 60. The Crohn's had just gone untreated for too long, he said. The damage had been done.

Amusingly, the Board of Bar Examiners did not believe me when I called the next morning to inform them that I was missing the bar exam for a bowel obstruction. They believed, perhaps not unreasonably, that *no one* would be so unlucky as to have a bowel obstruction the night before the bar exam, and I had therefore merely overslept. It was not until I provided my medical records and their own medical consultant had confirmed what happened that they finally understood I was telling the truth. Six months later, when I finally took the exam, the bar examiners were still suspicious; one of the proctors, concerned that the antiseizure and anti-inflammatory steroid medications I had taken with me to the test site were actually prohibited performance enhancing drugs, opened my pill bottles and swallowed a prednisone. I don't know what happened to him, but he left later that day.

Still, I passed. I hadn't wanted to be, and then I had been delayed by my own body, but I finally was a lawyer.

REBELLION

What happens to a dream deferred?

Does it dry up
like a raisin in the sun?
Or fester like a sore—
And then run?
Does it stink like rotten meat?
Or crust and sugar over—
like a syrupy sweet?

Maybe it just sags
like a heavy load.

Or does it explode?

— LANGSTON HUGHES, *HARLEM*

FOURTEEN

I was 26 years old when I almost died. And in that moment, I was finally born.

Two years earlier, I had passed the bar exam in 2013, found a niche working for Ashley's father, representing tenants facing eviction and suing slumlords. It was difference-making work, but he did it for profit rather than for the morality of it, and that meant if he were paid enough, he'd represent a landlord, too. Ashley was still hitting me, only her apologies had long since ended. Now, she'd just hit me if I looked at her the wrong way, squeeze my head if her dinner were not cooked to her liking, punch me in the back if the smoke alarm in our apartment building went off in the middle of the night. More than once she held a knife to my throat and told me she'd kill me if I ever tried to leave her, and at least a dozen times she'd held the knife to her own throat and said if I tried to leave she'd kill herself. I was more scared of *that* than I was of her threats against me.

In truth, Ashley had read me perfectly when we'd started dating. I had little to no support system, an abusive family, and she had offered me a way out. In my naïveté, I'd taken it without question. I had been the perfect mark. When she was diagnosed with bipolar disorder in our second year of marriage, I thought this meant her outbursts weren't her fault, and thus decided to let them go. She played into this beautifully, replacing her apologies with, "You know I can't control myself, it just happens" whenever one of her rage episodes ended.

In truth, her bipolar wasn't the cause of her rages, but her refusal to take her medication – she enjoyed the feeling of mania and didn't want to lose it – didn't help matters. During manic episodes, she'd lovebomb me, swearing undying love and promising she'd never hit me again. But when the inevitable crash came, I became the root of all evils in her life. She'd call me the worst mistake of her life, hit me with pots and pans, throw her shoes at me, hold a knife at my throat.

And still I never fought back.

For years, I had feared becoming my mother. I had feared her anger, her rage, her prejudice and bigotry, the way she harmed other people without a second thought. Even despite my male natal puberty, I still had my mother's slight frame and high cheekbones and I *looked* like her, which was yet another reason I grew a beard. I feared coming out, I feared transitioning, because if I looked like my mother, would I become her? I had hurt people too – with leaving Elaina behind, with parroting my mother's antiabortion lies and lines, with her Zionism, with checking the "other" box on my applications to college and law school. Was I already like her? These fears haunted me like demons, always in my mind. My nightly dreams had morphed; now interspersed with the forest was my childhood home, my mother ready with another pitcher of vinegar, telling me that we were alike. In my dreams, she'd waterboard me with the vinegar until I admitted we were the same. Then I'd wake up in a cold sweat.

I had decided early in our relationship that Ashley's treatment of me was a just punishment for what I'd done. If I was being hurt myself, I could not hurt anyone else. I was terrified of hurting any more people, so I became that most detestable of creatures: the political moderate. I decided that if I took the middle ground on every issue, I could not hurt anyone. It was an illogical decision based solely from fear. And so I spent my early twenties a quisling, meek and timid, unwilling to take any stands. I was exactly the opposite of my childhood self, and that filled me with shame, so I felt I deserved even more punishment. It was an endless shame cycle. And still my true self, my girl self, remained hidden, because the shame from that was worst of all, even as I hid women's underwear under my clothes. I had tried coming out to one therapist in 2014, asking him for next steps, but he unexpectedly passed away later that week before we could talk again. I took that as a sign.

In a display of just how meek I was, Ashley decided shortly after my graduation from law school to get an MBA from North Park University. Unwilling to do the schoolwork herself and knowing that I had been valedictorian at McDaniel, she instructed me to write all of her essays for her. The one time I refused, she threw a shoe at my head; as I ducked, it thudded into the wall so hard that it left a hole in the drywall.

"The next one won't miss," she said coldly.

I wrote her essays for her. She graduated with honors. She didn't stop hitting me with her fists, kitchen knives, an iron skillet. I wore long sleeve shirts even in summer to cover the bruises and cuts. Every day she would hit me in a different place, and then every day she would tell me it was my fault. One time I tried to assuage her anger by taking her to a Kohler spa for the day. On our way there, she was so angry that the package I'd purchased for her wasn't all inclusive package that she slammed my head into the steering wheel of the car, nearly causing us to drive off the road. Another time, upset that her dinner was not what she'd wanted – I did most of the cooking – she threw the full plate of food at my head. The plate shattered against the wall. Still another time, she kicked me out of our bedroom because my friend Matt had come to visit and she said I wasn't allowed to have friends over. When I tried talking to Matt in the second bedroom, she broke down the door– as in literally, she kicked the door off of its hinges – grabbed my phone out of my hand, and beat me with it.

"It's your fault for provoking me," she would say after each instance. "You know I can't control my temper, but you insist on provoking me. I think you must like making me feel like this."

In my terror of becoming my mother, I had ironically become my father: a weak person unwilling to stand up for myself, who would rather experience pain than run the risk of making things worse.

Thus, I was driving my Hyundai Elantra home from work one day in 2015, listening to the same song over and over again, in my usual depressed mood. The song, ironically enough, was Anna Nalick's "Breathe (2 AM)", which I'd sing over and over again:

> But you can't jump the track, we're like cars on a cable/
> And life's like an hourglass glued to the table/
> No one can find the rewind button now/
> Sing it if you understand.[i]

And in my depression I thought the song was telling me that I can't go back and change my life, that I'd missed my shot at being the girl I truly was, that the best I could hope for was simply not doing any more harm. Happiness would have required a different childhood, different choices. I had made my bed, I had to lie in it.

The car ahead of me was a large SUV; I saw its lights flash on as it braked, and pressed the brake pedal to follow suit.

Nothing happened.

I pressed the brake pedal harder. Still nothing. I planted both of my feet on the brake pedal with all of my strength, inches away from the SUV. *Still* nothing.

It's become a cliché that your life flashes before your eyes when you are about to die. It's become, ironically enough, equally a cliché that your life *doesn't* flash before your eyes. And on that summer day as my Elantra plowed into the back of the SUV ahead of me, as I sat, feet futilely planted against the brake pedal, hands braced on the steering wheel, everything slowed down around me. And what flashed before me, what I saw, was not my life, but my death.

I was about to die a lie. I had spent the last six years living a lie, and now I was about to die as one.

The Elantra's front bumper was too low to impact the bumper of the SUV ahead of me. The hood slipped underneath the bumper of the SUV and began to buckle. I saw the hood fold and contort as metal fragments flew towards my face. The check engine light flashed on. Glass shattered in the windshield as the engine compartment crumpled under the SUV, and I realized that the SUV was rising onto the rapidly collapsing forward section of the Elantra, and its bumper was headed towards me, and as soon as it collided with the cracking glass of the windshield my existence would be over.

I pictured my funeral. Ashley would be there crying. My parents would be there. They'd all sanitize my story and talk about the husband, the son, the meek and submissive and timid person who did whatever he was told and never challenged anything. I'd be remembered for my lack of integrity. For my fear. For what I'd been beaten into. It was like a bad joke. *I* was a bad joke. I had spent all my time trying to avoid becoming my mother, and what I had become instead was my father: a sad, pathetic, weak person, living a lie, too afraid to stand up to anyone to make a difference, letting other people do harm because I was too fearful to stop them.

My right knee slammed into the steering column; I felt something tear inside and a stabbing pain as it began to bleed. The airbags never deployed, so I saw my head as it finally collided with the steering wheel. Blood stung my eyes from somewhere above them on my forehead after the impact. The bumper of the SUV was mere inches away from the windshield now.

I closed my eyes and waited for the end. And in that moment, I realized for the first time just how lucky I had been in my life. Not lucky as in *blessed*, though certainly I'd had my share of blessings. Lucky as in *had luck*. I'd gone to college instead of being enlisted because of a flukey high SAT score, because I'd happened to be born to a middle class white family. I could have died from Crohn's Disease, but because I lived five minutes from a hospital when my intestine swelled shut, they had an NG tube inserted within thirty minutes and saved my life. I had a photographic memory, an uncanny ability to remember what I read. I had escaped my parents' abuse.

Thanks to my parents, I knew what suffering felt like. But unlike so many other people who were suffering, I had been given the ability – a college degree, a *law* degree and license, a photographic memory, white privilege – to do something about it for other people who were also suffering. And what had I done with it? And suddenly I felt ashamed not for what I had done, but for what I had *not* done. I hadn't even had the courage to tell people who I really was. I had a freaking law license, and I was going to die a lie.

I opened my eyes. I was crying now – not because I was going to die, but because I had wasted my life. I had been given so many gifts, and I had wasted them all.

I'd had Anna Nalick's song all wrong. It's not an acceptance that you had your chance and now must live with the consequences. It wasn't a peon to the justness of punishment. It's a reminder time is fleeting and you only have so many chances before they run out, and until that happens you have to live each moment as though it *is* your last chance. Your last chance is the one in the moment you are about to live, not the one in the moment that just ended.

The bumper of the SUV touched the windshield, stopped, started forwards again. The Elantra slid backwards, and the back of the SUV fell onto the pavement.

I was still alive.

There was no power in the Elantra's cabin; none of the lights or the dashboard worked. I tried opening the driver's side door, found it stuck. With great difficulty, my head fuzzy, my knee throbbing, I reached over, tried the passenger side door, and forced it open, then climbed outside. My right knee buckled and I fell onto the pavement, pulled myself up with my arms, then struggled to my feet.

The front of the Elantra was completely destroyed. The headlights were gone. Smoke rose from what had once been an engine bay; engine parts lay all over the road. There was no power to the car because the battery lay in the street; it had been shorn from the car in the accident. The SUV was relatively undamaged, with only the bumper showing any signs of being in a collision at all.

I'd suffered a concussion in the accident, but for all of the fuzziness in my head, my mind was clearer than it had been in years. My knee throbbed from a torn meniscus and ligaments that, thanks to my Crohn's Disease, could not be safely surgically repaired. The doctors told me my knee would be in pain for the rest of my life; the goal was simply to ensure that my knee could hold my weight so I could walk. I spent six months in physical therapy until my knee could support my weight without buckling. For most of that time, I walked with a cane. It didn't matter. I had been given a second chance. The thing about luck is that once you recognize it, once you recognize how much of your own life happened because of things completely out of your control, you realize just how much you owe to other people.

Two months later, I sat down with Ashley and asked her if she'd ever had dreams about being a man. Of course she hadn't, and she told me as such. And then I told her the truth. I found a gender therapist that same week. Within a year, I had started hormone replacement therapy.

FIFTEEN

Transitioning is not easy. First, I had to find a gender therapist who was willing to work with me. The first I met with was convinced that I wasn't actually trans, but just wanted to be a less fucked up version of my mother as some kind of coping mechanism. The second told me that I should wait until I was 60 to transition in order to live authentically in the final days before I died. But I had faced death twice now, and I had no further interest in living a lie. I didn't really need a therapist to tell me what I'd always known: that I was female, and always had been.

That's not to say I wasn't afraid. Truthfully, I was terrified. I was afraid that I'd waited too long, that no one would take me seriously as a woman. I was afraid that the world would consist mostly of people like my mother. I was afraid that my mother had been correct, that I really was an abomination. Some of my fears were valid; when I told Ashley's father, my boss, that I was transitioning, he thought it was a practical joke and started laughing. Dr. Scott, who had walked me down the aisle when I married Ashley, the closest remaining relationship I had to family, thought I'd betrayed her. Dr. Scott had thought of me like a son, and couldn't accept me as her daughter; to her, I had *killed* her son. Dr. Scott continued speaking with Ashley, though, and Ashley increasingly thought of herself as a "trans widow," whose husband had been killed by her now wife.

It wasn't just losing friends. The very first day I left our apartment in women's clothes, I went to a Walgreens pharmacy for a couple of grocery items. Another shopper mocked me as "a man wearing women's pants" and then excitedly ran about the store telling everyone he saw that a "crossdresser" was there and demanding to see a manager. Soon he escalated to demanding the police be called, and I left in tears.

Yet I had lived a lie for too long, and the more I learned about the transitioning process, the more I understood that this was something I *needed* to do for my own survival. This was the fix I had needed when I was a child, the fix I did not know had existed, the fix I had been denied in favor of conversion therapy and waterboarding. And I was lucky, too, to have a couple of mentors who guided me through the process. Kliff Svatos, a trans man who is still someone I'm proud to call a friend to this day, helped me with advice and as a sounding board and listened to my fears over and over again. The first day we met for lunch, he gave me advice I've never forgotten.

"If you're transitioning to fix everything in your life," he said, "don't do it. It doesn't work that way. But if you're transitioning because you need to transition, because you know it's who you are, then you should. If you're depressed before you transition, you'll still be depressed afterwards. But it's a lot easier to deal with that if you know who you are. That's what transitioning is for."

I knew what he was talking about. I had never thought being a girl would solve all of my problems. It was who I was, not a repair. When I finally got an appointment at Howard Brown's Chicago clinic to start the process, I didn't even read the consent forms before I signed them – a rarity for a famously deliberate lawyer who reads *everything* I sign. I had waited two decades for this. Still, the doctor made me read them before he'd take them back, and then verbally explained everything in detail – including the effects and risks – before asking me, "Are you sure you want to do this?"

I absolutely was. And the first time I injected myself with estrogen, I finally felt like me. For the first time in my life, I recognized a hint of myself in the mirror. Before that injection, I had been watching someone else's life through my own eyes. Now, I saw my own life. The best example I can give is watching The Wizard of Oz, when Judy Garland's Dorothy exits her ruined black-and-white house into a land of color. I'm profoundly colorblind, yet HRT had that effect on me.

Those mental changes were far more important – and more profound – than any physical changes. Certainly, some of the physical effects were greatly welcomed; between the HRT and a dozen sessions of laser, I lost most of my facial hair, and fat deposits migrated to new places. My skin softened. Yet my breasts never grew beyond small B-cups (much to my chagrin). More important was the end of the male features that had tortured me, more than any waterboarding, since the onset of natal puberty. The involuntary erections that had plagued me for a decade and a half finally ended, and I was able to finally stop trying to cut off my penis every day – for yes, those efforts had never stopped. I had never had an orgasm before HRT, mostly because the very thought of sex with a male organ disgusted me. Now, with HRT and therapy, as my brain remapped itself, I actually orgasmed for the first time.

Transition is so much more than medical. I had to pick a new name, as my deadname was simply not going to work any longer. I strongly considered "Jane," the name I'd given myself as a little girl, as well as "Tasha," after the character who'd prompted my first epiphany. Yet true to my eminently practical form, I elected instead to select a name with more continuity, one that would let me keep my initials. I figured that would make transferring the more mundane aspects of my life a bit easier. After a few experiments – "Samara Meredith" was a runner up –

I settled on "Sheryl Melanie," because it means "darling of the darkness." It seemed to fit me. I had, after all, always been a creature beloved by the dark.

With the mental changes came more confidence. I shed the moderate persona, increasingly allowing my inner moral compass more leash. I joined the Democratic Socialists of America. I went back to the Walgreens where I'd been chased out before. I challenged Ashley's father more and more, demanding he take more *pro bono* cases, and taking some of my own when he was out of the office. And I told Ashley to stop hitting me. I was rapidly growing confidence because I felt, for the first time in my life, *like me*. I wasn't watching someone else's life through my eyes anymore; now I was more and more *living*. And I liked it.

At first, Ashley had been supportive of my transition, even taking me for a makeup lesson and accompanying me shopping for outfits. She had talked of getting our hair done together, our nails done together. And for a while, I thought things might improve. Yet as I progressed, as I became less of a shrinking violet and more sure of myself, she became more resistant. She began openly talking about how much she missed my pre-transition self, the one who wouldn't tell her to stop hitting me. And her rages became more frequent and more pronounced – and more violent.

One weekend, about a year after I started hormones, Ashley became enraged when I was giving myself my hormone injection. I tried to leave, to walk away, but she wasn't having it. She grabbed me, put her hands around my throat, choking me, and threw me against a wall in the hallway. With her face mere centimeters from mine, she snarled that this was my fault – that my transition was simply a way to get her angry so she would hit me, and therefore feel bad about herself. I gasped and struggled for air, still unwilling to fight back; meeting violence with violence would only lead to more violence, and I didn't want to hurt her any more than I already had. I'd hurt enough people in my life.

"Do you enjoy this? Huh? You must really like what you do to me!" Ashley screamed. Her grip lessened momentarily, and I peeled her hands off my throat, ran into the guest bedroom in our two bedroom apartment, closed and locked the door. I gasped for breath.

Ashley called afterwards that she was throwing my hormones down the toilet. And something in me snapped.

I'm not going back, came the voice in my head. I had lost too much. I was not losing my fragile womanhood too. I heard the sound of a toilet flush, presumably carrying my estrogen into the sewer. I heard footsteps. And then I heard a loud thud outside the locked bedroom door. Ashley was trying to break in.

I panicked. I was a woman and no one could take that away from me. I would die before I detransitioned. Experiencing a year of being my true self only to lose it now was a cruel joke. *I was not going back*. My pretransition self was a quarter century nightmare that I had barely survived. No one was taking my womanhood from me.

The thud came again, louder. The wood trim around the door began to crack. "Let me in," Ashley shrieked. "I'll kill you!"

I didn't have my phone, but I did have my laptop. I sent MaTt a Facebook message to call 911.

Another thud. Another crack. Ashley was making greater and greater threats, accusing me of forcing her to hurt me. I had reached my breaking point, where I would risk it all. My seizure medication was in the guest bedroom; I slept there so often – kicked out of the master bedroom by Ashley – that I kept my nighttime medications there instead. I opened the bottle and downed the pills.

All of them.

I wasn't dying by Ashley's hand, and I was not detransitioning. Either I would die on my own terms or I would go to the hospital where they would give me my estrogen. If this was the only choice I had left, I would make it. The seizure medicine was oxcarbazepine, a type of benzodiazepine; I'd just go to sleep. I'd get to die a woman. If I had nothing else, no one could take that away from me.

Ashley broke down the door as the paramedics arrived.

For all of Ashley's claims about being unable to control her anger, that wasn't always the case. True, she routinely hit me, screamed at me, shoved me in restaurants, malls, grocery stores. Sometimes she'd be so brazen about it that someone would mouth or whisper "are you okay?" at me. But in front of police officers or first responders, in front of people she feared, her anger would dissipate remarkably quickly. And so, when the first responders knocked on the door – the police, the fire department, the paramedics – Ashley answered them coolly, informing them nothing was wrong. She hadn't known Matt had called them. Yet the paramedics saw the broken door, asked me if I was okay. And I told them that I'd swallowed a bottle of seizure medicine, needed to go to the hospital.

Ashley was furious. It didn't matter. The paramedics scooped me up, took me to the hospital. I had the benzos pumped from my system, and then I spoke in the emergency room with a social worker who asked me what had happened.

I told her the truth. She asked me if I was safe, and I told her no. She asked if I wanted to be admitted to the psychiatric ward of the hospital on suicide watch, and I said yes – not because I would try to kill myself again, but because I needed to get away from Ashley so I didn't. Ashley, upon learning I was being admitted, sobbed and begged me to come home instead. But I no longer trusted her. I'd seen how far she was willing to go.

And truthfully, I needed help. I needed to stabilize my fragile self where I could fight for myself safely. I needed a plan to get away from her. I was done being abused. I just had no idea where to start.

I SPENT a full week in the psychiatric hospital. The staff was for the most part incredibly accommodating of having a trans patient, letting me have my own room and access to my makeup bag every morning. They let me shave my legs, face, and armpits as long as someone watched me to make sure I wouldn't try to kill myself again. The deal the nurses and therapists made with me, however, was that I needed to honestly tell them what had happened and how they could help me. And so I did.

I had started dating Ashley mere months after I moved out of my parents' house. That meant that the psych ward was, in a very real sense, the first time in my life I felt completely safe. No one was going to waterboard me or hit me or try to kill me. No one would call me an abomination and no one would tell me I was better off dead. I was safer for that week in a psych ward than I was at any previous time in my life. And so for the first time in my life I could breathe.

Thus, in a strange way, the stay at the psych ward was the first week of the rest of my life. There is in my mind a clear dividing line between my life before that hospitalization and afterwards. Being in a psych ward was like living in a bubble. Days and nights blend together; hours feel like days and days feel like months. I gave makeup lessons to the other girls on my floor who wanted to know how to blend their foundation better. I talked about my life in group therapy sessions, for the first time revealing to anyone what my childhood had been like. I talked about being hit by Ashley and being scared that all I would ever be was a punching bag. I talked about my lifelong desire to help people, that I wanted something more for myself. It's weird to say I liked it there but… to that point, it was the best part of my life.

The first day I was there, I locked eyes with a young trans man who was also there. We were the only two trans patients on the floor, so we spent a lot of time together the first couple of days we were there. He was a few years younger than me; I was already 27, but he was barely 21. He was an artist of truly special talent; he'd sketch pictures of truly amazing quality. I knew he was smitten with me when he sketched me on my third day there.

Truth be told, the feeling was mutual.

Ashley had been my first girlfriend, my first date, my first sexual and romantic relationship. And after she'd started hitting me, I'd stayed because I was trapped. It would be lying to say I had no feelings for her, because I did. And having feelings for a person who hits you, who denigrates you, who runs you down, is a mindfuck.

But this boy, who had beautiful features and a soft blond beard and said my name like an incantation, put me on a pedestal. We made eyes at each other across the group therapy sessions. He talked to me about his plans for the future and his art and I liked the way his long hair reminded me of the hero from a fantasy movie. He said I was beautiful.

Even after learning all I had done. He listened to my story in group therapy sessions, heard my litany of sins. And still.

He said *I* was beautiful.

And he said it like a prayer, as though I were some sort of goddess. I didn't understand why; no one had ever called me beautiful before, and I wasn't exactly a looker. But here he was, with his Legolas hair and five o'clock shadow and smoky voice and artistic hands saying that *I* was beautiful. I wanted to kiss him, wanted him to kiss me, in my mind begged him to kiss me. We never got the opportunity. We flirted, but the ever present staff made sure it never went farther.

He got out a couple of days before I did. When we hugged as he left, he picked me up and twirled me around and I laughed like a schoolgirl. I lived a lifetime during that embrace. And for the next two days, in that strange bubble world of the psych ward, where everything was possible, I dreamt of a future with him, where I could have gotten out and been with him.

When I got out two days later, an email from him was waiting for me. In it, he confessed he really had fallen in love with me during our time in the weird timeless bubble that is a psychiatric hospital. And for the briefest of moments, I considered throwing everything away, writing and confessing that I loved him back, that he had taught me I really was capable of being loved. And I typed out a message telling him as much.

And then I deleted it.

Putting aside that we had met literally in a *psychiatric hospital*, I was both *married* and several years older than him. If we had been ten years older, the age difference might not have been so significant, but 27 and not yet 21 meant we were in completely different places in our lives. Plus, as tempting as he was, as much as I wanted him, I wasn't going to cheat on Ashley, because that would have been wrong. And I wasn't about to ask him to wait for me, because I had no idea how long it was going to take to get away from her.

But most of all, following him, following my heart, would have been putting him in danger, because I knew what Ashley was capable of. I would have been risking his safety for my own selfishness.

So I deleted what I had typed out. And in its place, I told him that I was married, that this wasn't going to work, that he shouldn't contact me again.

And then I cried for hours.

But I owe him a debt of gratitude. What he taught me was that I was lovable, that I *could* be loved as something more than a punching bag. He taught me that I deserved better. And in the psych ward, in his arms as he twirled me, I resolved to leave Ashley, to leave all the abusive people behind, to treat myself as someone who deserved to be loved.

To treat myself the way he would have treated me.

In the years since I left the psych ward, I have often thought about him. At first, I feared I was unlovable. I despaired that in my zeal to do the right thing, to do the moral thing, I had cost myself my only chance at happiness. But at the same time, I could not accept that if I was lovable by him, I was lovable *only* by him. Maybe one day I could even be lovable by myself, even if it took a lifetime of work to get there.

It took two years of preparation to leave Ashley. I told only a handful of people lest they alert Ashley ahead of time. Ashley had long warned me that if I left she would kill me, so I waited to file for divorce until after she had gone to her mother's for a few days, and included a petition for an order of protection with my filing. But I did it, after years of preparation.

I had to set up my own bank account in secret, get a car in solely my name, get my own apartment, all without her finding out. The hitting continued through all of that time. One week-end, about six months after the psych ward, Ashley hit me so hard that a neighbor called the police about the noise that had occurred when the back of my head hit the wall. When the police arrived, Ashley told the officers frankly that she was hitting me because I was trans, and she wanted her husband back.

The officer nodded, took some notes, then walked over to me. I was holding a cloth to my still-bleeding head.

"Is your transition complete? Is it permanent?" he asked, pointing to my genitals. "Because if it isn't, I think you should just stop. That would make her happy, and then you don't get hit any more. I wish all of my calls were this easy."

The end of my marriage to Ashley meant that for the first time in my life, I *lived*. I started getting tattoos, a way to reclaim my body from my Crohn's, from my mother. My first ever tattoo was a quote from John Muir: "Into the forest I go, to lose my mind and find my soul." I had it tattooed on my rib cage so I could feel the pain and know I was still alive, that I had won, that this body was mine and it was beautiful. And in place of the comma, I added a semicolon, to symbolize the suicide attempts I had survived.

Ashley's father fired me for "not consulting [him] in [my] decision to transgender," but that was fine by me; I got a job with a legal aid clinic representing people in eviction court for free. I loved that job, I loved the work, and I loved my coworkers, and I was heartbroken when the Covid-19 pandemic caused the clinic to close a few years later. But the best part of that job was meeting Sahreen.

Sahreen and her husband lived in a condominium building in Wheeling, Illinois, being taken over by a large company thanks to a racist, classist quirk in Illinois law that allowed corporations to force condo owners to sell at a price of the corporation's choosing, a process called "condominium deconversions." These deconversions typically targeted buildings where the owners were immigrants, Black, or Indigenous people. I had represented people in this situation before, so when the folks at the Wheeling condo building needed a lawyer to defend them, my clinic took their case. There wasn't a legal means to stop the sale, but we could extract financial concessions and force the company to at least pay above market and ensure that no one walked away owing money on their mortgages. Sahreen and I became friends during that process, and after the case was over, she came to work at the legal clinic too. She remains my best friend to this day and is very much my chosen sister.

When the time came for gender confirmation surgery, there was a problem. My Crohn's meant that a vaginoplasty was out of the question; one surgeon told me there was a significant possibility I'd die on the operating table, and another told me that the autoimmune condition meant I would never be able to properly heal. Every medical opinion was the same: They could remove tissue, but building something new was simply not an option, not if I wanted to survive the surgery. So I told them to remove all that was removable, and leave it at that. At another point in my life, this could have killed me, set me into a spiral of depression from which I could never have emerged. But I didn't transition only to die. I transitioned to *live*, and this body which was my companion through life was a woman's body whether it had a vagina or not, because I had a woman's soul. I had always known that to be true.

Three years after I was discharged from the psychiatric hospital, I met the most beautiful woman I'd ever seen, with dark eyes set against caramel skin and a smile that made me weak in the knees. I knew she was out of my league from the first time I laid eyes on her, but all the same we talked seven hours on the phone and she dazzled me with talk of the Bernoulli principle, the physics behind flying, and the way that car transmissions work. The next day, we had our first date, and after hours more of talking, she smiled *that* smile and said yes when I asked if I could kiss her. Later that night, for the first time in my life, I invited someone to stay over on a first date. I had learned my lesson. I *was* lovable. I was going to let this gorgeous woman love me.

And that woman, the love of my life, my wife Mercedes, continues to do just that to this very day.

SIXTEEN

It was summer, two years after I'd started transitioning. I was well into my plans to leave Ashley, shed all abusers from my life, start fresh. I was in, of all places, a clothing store; Ashley worked there, and I was picking her up from work. Until I was safe and free and away from her, I didn't dare risk arousing suspicion by breaking routine. I knew all too well the consequences of that, and the consequences in my wrist still hurt when it rained. I walked around the little store, waiting for Ashley to finish vacuuming ahead of locking up for the night, humming to myself and browsing the racks for outfit inspiration.

My phone buzzed in the back pocket of my jeans; I'd received an email. Assuming it was from a client, I absent-mindedly grasped the device and opened my mail app.

It wasn't a client.

Elaina had emailed me. Our mother was in the hospital after what Elaina termed a "cardiac event." And she wanted to see me.

It had been an eventful few years for my mother. After my graduation from law school, my mother had gone back to school at, of all places, my alma mater: McDaniel College. She became, surprisingly enough, a child therapist, which prompted no shortage of sleepless nights for me when I thought about what she'd done to me, and now having access to vulnerable children in a therapeutic setting. I had reported her to the State of Maryland when I'd found out, hoping they'd think twice about letting an abuser be a child therapist, but my letter to the authorities there went unanswered.

And now she was sick, maybe dying, and wanted to see me.

My mind was racing. On some level, I'd always known this day would come eventually. Admittedly, I'd assumed it would be my mother's multiple sclerosis, rather than a heart attack, which would lead to the inevitable message. I briefly indulged in a moment of dark humor, and granted myself a chuckle at the thought – cliché though it may be – that my mother even *had* a heart. Then I felt guilty for downplaying what had to be terrifying for her. Her entire life had been about a lack of control, beginning with her relationship with my father and continuing through the loss of control of her body that came with MS. Even *I*, her trans daughter, had been just another example of something she could not control. And now she would be in a hospital bed, afraid, once again not in control. I thought back to my first hospitalization from Crohn's the night before the bar exam, and the half dozen more I'd had by that point since then, and I knew what she must be feeling.

And for the first time in my life, I felt a kinship with my mother. My lifelong fear about becoming my mother hid the reality that in some ways we actually were very much alike. This wasn't just in our similar features and appearance; what had been a strong resemblance before my transition had, after two years of HRT, become me essentially looking like a younger version of my mother in the mirror, albeit with brown eyes instead of green ones. And not in terms of morals or values either, for mine were the polar opposite of hers; that I could say as much with some degree of certainty admittedly brought me a sense of pride.

Instead, we both attempted to bring to heel that which we

could not control, because what we could not control frightened us. I had embarked on a quest to control injustice, to prevent homelessness, because the inability to control it frightened me. My mother shared that same fear, but where I sought to bring order to what I saw as unfair and inequitable, my mother sought to bring order in what she saw as immoral. From that certain point of view, we were not so different. The thing which divided us was simply what we saw as immoral. To my mother, it was interracial marriage, trans and queer identities, abortion, Palestinian people existing. To me, it was wealth inequality, racism, homophobia, and a lack of bodily autonomy.

So in that moment, standing in the clothing store, reading and rereading Elaina's email, I saw my mother as a human being for the first time since my early childhood. I saw her not as an omniscient, omnipotent, devilish figure, but a human being. A misguided human being. A scared, flawed, human being, whose fears had driven her to hate, to push away what she did not understand.

I started crying. Not because what she had done was okay. But because I understood it, and because of that understanding, I forgave her.

Years earlier, a therapist had attempted to get me angry about what my mother had done to me. He'd beseeched me to lash out, scream, yell, curse her existence, punch a wall. He'd even taken me into a room filled with breakable objects, handed me a large foam t-ball bat, and encouraged me to hit whatever I wanted. I'd refused.

"It's not constructive, and it won't change anything that happened," I'd said. "I don't like being angry. No one ever solved anything by being angry." True, anger was an emotion I'd always found foreign, unsettling, unless the anger was directed towards myself. But back then, even as I'd said the words and known their truth, I hadn't really understood *why* I felt that way.

Yet in the clothing store, I did. I couldn't be angry with my mother without being angry at myself, because what had made her what she was also made me what I was. We were strangely alike. It was a prospect that at once fascinated and frightened me. And for a brief, tantalizing moment, I considered going to her bedside, confronting her with the reality of her oldest daughter fully realized despite her best efforts. Maybe, just maybe, if she saw just how similar we really were, she could accept me.

But just as quickly as that thought came, it was gone. We were similar, yes. We were stubborn. We feared what we could not control and sought to control it anyway. But we were also different. My mother had turned that fear outward into trying to reshape her universe in her white and cisheteronormative image. I had turned my fear inward, using it as fuel to drive me to make the world better. And that distinction mattered. I was no saint, and I certainly was in no position to judge my mother. But did I really want her influence in my life? Would I want to be around a racist homophobe, even if she was my mother?

All of this went through my mind in the minutes I stood there. By the next morning, Elaina and I had exchanged a few emails. Three things were crystal clear: Elaina had never forgiven me. My mother wanted desperately to see me. And she also insisted that if I came to see her, I would need to detransition first. And I understood that our respective needs for control would never be compatible with each other.

My mother was still yearning for the son she wanted but never had. What she wanted was for me to put on an act for her peace of mind. Maybe her condition was serious. For all I knew, she was dying. And perhaps a better person than I would have been able to pretend, live the lie, for the length of a hospital visit. But in the final analysis, I was just like my mother. I was just as stubborn. And my identity wasn't a costume that could be donned and discarded at the drop of a hat. My dignity would not be subject to my mother's whims any longer.

I could forgive my mother. But I could not forgive myself if after everything I'd been through, everything she put me through, I did to myself what she had done to me. I was, for better or worse, her oldest daughter. Her oldest daughter would visit her in the hospital if she wanted to see me. The son who never was would not be available. Those were the terms, those would always be the terms, and they were non-negotiable.

And so, my heart pounding in my chest so loudly I could hear it, right there in the clothing store I wrote Elaina back, telling her that I would be willing to see our mother, but I would not detransition to do it – and I did not want a relationship with either of our parents.

Elaina and I ended up emailing back and forth a few times, and Sabrina joined the email conversation later that day. I wanted a relationship with them. I wanted them to meet their older sister, to be a part of their lives. I had a single condition: that whatever we talk about, whatever we discuss, stay between us. I did not want a relationship with our parents. Whatever my mother was, whatever she'd done to me, was inseparable from what my father had done to her, and that made him culpable too. Plus, I simply didn't want their brand of toxic, deep seated racism, Zionism, and homophobia in my life. Even putting aside what my parents had done to *me*, most of my friends were Black, Brown, disabled, Muslim, or queer. My parents simply weren't safe for them to be around.

But that condition was a nonstarter for my sisters. Sabrina had experienced a different childhood than I. The tension she had experienced growing up was the pressure of living up to her reputation as the golden child, constantly expected by our parents to eclipse me easily. She had a good relationship with our parents now and wanted to preserve it. To Sabrina, my demand to not have a relationship with them amounted to making her choose between us, and she would choose them.

Elaina, meanwhile, had been forced by my departure years earlier to preserve her relationship with them. And understandably, to her I was in no position to be making demands. In her mind, the least I could do was visit our mother in the hospital with no preconditions, even if that meant detransitioning first. It was a position borne from hardened necessity, concluded with a plea to do this for family peace, a last ditch effort to make our family whole again. I wouldn't even be given the address of the hospital unless I agreed.

But I had spent the first twenty years of my life trying to make the family whole whilst I was an empty husk. It had nearly killed me more than once. I had before me what was, at bottom, a zero sum game: Either my family would be whole or I would be. In retrospect, I perhaps could have lied, said I would detransition and then simply not. But that would have been flippant and disrespectful to myself, treating my identity like a costume when my life had demonstrated it was not. Who I am is not a bargaining chip.

I didn't go. And I never spoke with my sisters again.

SEVENTEEN

There is a belief that living in a blue state means safety for trans people. It is a myth shared by Democrats and Republicans alike: Republicans, to support their meritless assertions that Democratic states are bastions of immorality where children are forcibly transitioned *en masse,* Democrats, to absolve themselves from responsibility for the very real transphobia which exists in Democratic states. The reality is neither belief is true.

Despite Illinois' reputation as the California of the Midwest, my experience with Illinoisans upon coming out was not a universally pleasant one. In the condominium complex where Ashley and I lived, neighbors began taking pictures of me, creating slide shows that zoomed in on my chest and mocking my growing breasts. This sort of photography became a favorite pastime of the other people who lived in our building, to the point where I drew a small crowd for things like taking out the garbage or walking our chihuahua. Home was not a safe haven because of Ashley's abuse, but it also was a living nightmare to step foot outside.

But the dangers were more than gawkers. It took over a year

of hormones before I passed for cis to most people, but the "lived experience" requirements of the World Professional Association for Transgender Health (WPATH) guidelines – directives that a trans person live as their true gender for a period of time even before starting hormones – meant that I was clocked as trans long before that. One time, meeting a client in a coffee shop to discuss their case, I went to the women's restroom. The coffee shop had two restrooms, one each marked "men" and "women," and each was a one person facility with a single toilet and sink. In short, there was zero chance of me posing a danger to anyone using the women's restroom, because anyone using it would be by themselves. Of course, that didn't stop a crowd from gathering when I used the women's room, with several people banging on the door and demanding that I leave the restroom – and the coffee shop – immediately. Two people threatened to call the cops; several more called me a pervert.

It wasn't only private citizens. Transportation Security Administration ("TSA") agents made flights hellish, with strip searches a routine demand. One time, boarding a flight in Chicago to Washington D.C. for a work conference, a TSA agent asked me archly "What even *are* you?" before loudly asking her colleagues, "Do you know what *it* is?" By "it," she was of course referring to me. When I asked what she meant, she responded by repeating her question and telling me costumes weren't allowed on flights.

Doctors' appointments were perhaps worst of all. I had to find a new primary care doctor after the staff at my doctor's office began treating me as a curiosity – or worse. One day, during a routine checkup, the doctor's nurse, who came in to check my vitals, gleefully told me she'd requested me specifically because "I've always wanted to meet a drag queen!" When I tried explaining that trans people and drag performers were different, she paid no attention, instead (without permission) grabbing my breasts through my blouse and asking how I had gotten such realistic breast forms. They were, in point of fact, entirely my own.

Another time, I was at my gastroenterologist's office for an MRI, one of a battery of periodic tests I have to monitor the progression of my Crohn's Disease. The technician waited until I was in the MRI tube, unable to object, then began misgendering me through the speaker, calling me a "mentally ill man" and laughing at "what a freak" I was. Even after the test was over, he refused to let me out of the MRI tube, demanding I agree with him that I was just a sexually disturbed man or he would leave me there. What was supposed to be a half hour in the tube was over two hours as I refused to accede to his demand and he refused to let me out. He eventually let me out only when another technician asked him what the delay was as more patients were waiting.

Even doctors weren't immune from this kind of virulent transphobia. My neurologist, who was monitoring my seizures, flatly refused to continue to treat me unless I stopped my transition. Treating a trans patient, she said, was against her ethics, and she didn't want anyone in her practice with whose morality she disagreed.

OF ALL THE hardships I'd expected when I transitioned, the one I expected the least was the resistance of the legal profession. It's incredibly naïve in retrospect, but I had thought that Chicago, Illinois, a blue dot in a blue state, would be among the safest places to navigate being a transgender professional. It was a superb fantasy with no basis in reality whatsoever.

Shortly after I began hormones, I called the Attorney Registration and Disciplinary Commission (the "ARDC"), the Illinois government agency which regulates attorneys. (The ARDC is the Illinois equivalent of the state bar in most other states, and both licenses and disciplines attorneys.) The ARDC offers a hotline for attorneys with ethics questions, and I wanted to make sure that I complied with any applicable rules as I navigated the process. So cheerfully and with no idea of what I was starting, I called the ethics hotline, let the pleasant woman on the other side of the line know that I was trans and would be transitioning publicly, and asked her if there was anything I needed to be sure I did to comply with the ethics rules. The people who operate the ethics hotline aren't allowed to give their names, so I have no idea who she was.

"No one has ever asked us that before," said the woman. "But let me ask my boss and I will call you back."

A few hours later, she did just that.

"I'm afraid I have some bad news," she told me. The ARDC does not allow attorneys to be transgender, she explained, because otherwise attorneys who are facing discipline like disbarment would simply transition to avoid punishment.

I was flabbergasted.

"I'm pretty sure if someone is facing disbarment their first phone call won't be to an endocrinologist," I said in disbelief. But she wasn't done. The ARDC wouldn't permit me to change my name or transition, because they believed doing so would violate the ethics rules governing attorneys. If I did so, she said, I would face discipline up to and including being disbarred.

I spent the next seven years fighting for my license.

Despite the ARDC's warnings, I decided to move forward. I had been on hormones long enough that I couldn't simply stop, and I wasn't about to prioritize my license over my life. I couldn't go back in the closet; I had lived that lie for far too long already. I had my name and gender marker legally changed, but still the ARDC refused to let me change either on the master rolls of attorneys. The result was that even after a year of HRT – which meant I passed for cis to the overwhelming majority of people – I had no choice but to identify myself by my deadname in court, and thereby immediately out myself.

The result wasn't just humiliation or embarrassment. Judges, upon learning I was trans, were overtly hostile at best. One judge at the Daley Center in Chicago refused to refer to me using she/her pronouns and when I asked for a third time for him to do so, he responded archly "I'm wearing the robe, I will call you what I want." He then proceeded to use male pronouns to refer to me another fourteen times during the hearing, threatening to hold me in contempt when I objected again.

It wasn't only judges. Opposing lawyers began filing motions to disqualify me from cases, saying it violated their religious freedom to have to litigate against me. More than a few were granted. One arbitration panel, faced with such a motion, held that people are either male or female based on their gender assigned at birth; as such, they concluded I was not a person and my client was unrepresented, and ruled summarily in favor of the other side. Another tribunal held that transness was a mental illness which proved that I was not capable of practicing law, and disqualified me on that basis. Few, if any, lawyers used she/her pronouns for me in court. One lawyer even filed a motion asking a court to declare me male, saying, "LGBTQ+ activists have no place in the law" and "here we deal with reality and facts, not fantasy." All of these cases were landlord-tenant cases where I represented the tenant or family cases where I was representing an indigent party; not one of these cases had anything to do with my gender identity until opposing counsel brought it up.

But these were only the tip of the iceberg. Outside of Cook County, things were even worse. In one county, opposing counsel filed a motion for sanctions against me, asking the court to order me to pay their attorney fees for transitioning. Another lawyer told me he would never refer to me as a woman because "that's not how I was raised" and told the judge that my gender identity was a "cheap trick" to win the case. Several lawyers asked judges to order me to wear men's clothes to court, which wasn't possible after years of HRT anyway. Halfway through an all-day mediation, one judge ended proceedings and ordered me to remain, then spent the next four hours asking me probing questions about whether my gender identity was the result of sexual abuse, whether I needed psychiatric help, and finally demanded to inspect my genitalia.

That wasn't the only time a judge demanded a genital inspection from me. After I came out, lawyers and judges alike developed a fascination with my genitals, and genital inspections became a routine demand from judges. Some were simply chasers, who wanted a sexual experience with a trans person and were perfectly willing to leverage their positions on the bench to obtain it. One judge proposed a threesome with opposing counsel right in the courtroom upon learning I was trans, and frankly invoked their desire to experience "the best of both worlds." I consistently refused these advances, but doing so was frequently detrimental to my clients.

This forced me into an impossible position. For most of these incidents, there was no court reporter present (court reporters usually must be paid for by the party ordering the reporter, and representing indigent clients meant that's money I simply didn't have), and that meant my word against that of the judge – a contest I learned the hard way I simply could not win. Another judge at the Daley Center in eviction court *sua sponte* (on her own motion) ruled against my clients and in favor of the landlord, concluding that trans people could not be trusted because our existence is lying about our gender and therefore a fraud upon the court. When I filed a motion to disqualify that judge on grounds of her bias, a second judge hearing that motion frankly told me she agreed with the first judge, and opined that most judges agreed with her.

"Are you going to file a motion to disqualify me too?" she asked sarcastically.

Thus, for years, I would have to tell prospective clients that I was transgender and that my gender identity may be a deciding factor in their cases. More than one asked me to detransition for their case, and each time I politely but firmly refused. Many, unwilling to take the risk, decided to represent themselves or seek other counsel. One client, after witnessing a judge's hostile demeanor towards my transness in open court, accused me of being a child molester.

"There's no other reason he would treat you like that. He's a judge. You must be a groomer," she said. My protestations otherwise were useless.

After almost a year of spinning my wheels and accomplishing nothing, my conversations with the ARDC reached an uneasy truce: They would not discipline me for practicing law whilst trans, and I would not report the transphobia I saw on a daily basis. I even was finally able to have my name changed on the master roll of attorneys, though the ARDC continued to publicly list my deadname along with my legal name on its website. That meant any Google search of my name revealed both, and people took complete advantage.

The Winnebago County Circuit Clerk continued to list my cases under my deadname for years after my name was legally changed, meaning that in the court system, my cases would be called by my deadname. Each time I visited the courthouse, I went to the court clerk's office and asked for my name to be changed in the system. Each time, I was told that wasn't possible. And so I continued to be outed every time I had a case in Winnebago County, month after month, year after year.

After one particularly bad day, where I had not been properly gendered a single time during four different hearings, I'd had enough. The entire process was humiliating. I wasn't Clarence Darrow or Ketanji Brown Jackson, of course, but I was still a pretty good lawyer – a lawyer who couldn't do her job because all judges and opposing counsel wanted to discuss was my genitals. In despair, sobbing uncontrollably, I decided to leave the law.

Ironically, although going to law school had been something I'd done for my mother rather than myself, part of my futile

quest to make her proud of me, I'd actually grown rather
attached to my career. It wasn't the actual lawyering part, and it
certainly wasn't the money; consumer law and eviction defense
aren't exactly lucrative, and after my move to legal aid cut an
already meager salary in half, I could barely paid my rent (and
rarely pay it on time). But I had the ability to help people who
otherwise would go unrepresented, to save people's homes and
livelihoods, and sometimes even their lives. It was a great feeling
when the judge would ignore my gender identity, follow the law,
and dismiss an eviction case against my client.

But leaving the law felt wrong for another reason as well. It
felt like I was being forced out. I wasn't leaving on my terms. I
was leaving because I was being tortured, treated like a labora-
tory experiment or a sexual object. I was leaving because being
trans made me a liability to my clients, made them more likely to
lose because it put me in the position of either agreeing to whatever was demanded of me, being subjected to genital inspections
or a hundred questions about my background, or losing my
client's case. I had no dignity.

And so I applied to social work school, was accepted, and set
a hard deadline to leave the law at the end of that year. In an
online support group for trans people, I announced my decision.
One of the other members was a trans kid, not yet a teenager,
who wanted to be a lawyer when they grew up. And they
responded by asking whether, when they became a lawyer, they
would have to go through the same treatment.

The question stopped me cold.

I was running away. And because I was running away, the
next generation of trans people would have it harder. I had the
ability to take some of the arrows now so they wouldn't have to
later.

From that point forward, I refused to deadname or
misgender myself in court. The transphobia only worsened. Each
year I proposed a rule change to allow trans people to practice
law under our preferred names, pronouns, and gender markers,

and each year, it had been ignored. I went up the proverbial ladder at the ARDC, pleading my case for a more inclusive and less transphobic policy governing trans and gender noncon-forming lawyers. I was rebuffed at every turn. When I reported opposing counsel and judges for their transphobia, I was told flatly they were not violating any rules – but by practicing law whilst trans, *I* was. During one conversation with a high ranking official at the ARDC, I explained that having self-identification pronoun options and preventing deadnaming were basics of trans inclusion. The official countered that she had asked a cis gay employee if the ARDC's policy was transphobic, and he had said no, so I was obviously wrong. In a different conversation with another high ranking ARDC lawyer later that year, when the ARDC added a "non-binary" option to its annual registration form, I pointed out that the addition didn't mean much if the only thing non-binary attorneys gained by self-identifying would be getting harassed and misgendered in court. In response, I was told that a cis gay consultant had informed the agency that "non-binary" and "transgender" were synonymous, and any legal protections for trans lawyers would run afoul of the freedom of speech rights for cis lawyers.

So finally, with nowhere else to turn, I sued the Winnebago County Circuit Clerk for deadnaming me. At the first hearing, Judge Celia Gamrath, one of the best judges I've ever had the privilege of practicing before, archly informed the Clerk's counsel that this was a problem that should be "remedied in short order." And, to my legitimate surprise, it was; within two weeks after that hearing, the Circuit Clerk had updated its records and my name and pronouns were now correct. My lawsuit had achieved in two months what years of polite requests had not. I had proven that it was possible to fight trans-phobia in court and win.

By this point, Mercedes and I were living together and engaged to be married. She had watched me be misgendered and deadnamed in court, by this point six years after I had begun publicly transitioning. She had watched me write to the ARDC for help. She had read my proposed rule changes. She had seen my distraught face when my requests and proposals were ignored. So she wasn't surprised when I had sued the Winnebago County Circuit Clerk.

Most people would have taken the victory over the Circuit Clerk and run with it. Yet I couldn't. The last few years percolated in my mind, and just winning this one case was frankly not enough. I knew judges would continue to deadname and misgender me. I knew attorneys would continue to file motions to disqualify me.

By this time, the legal aid clinic was gone, shuttered by the Covid-19 pandemic. Not wanting my clients there to go without representation, I had started a "pay what you can," "name your own price" law practice, working with nonprofits to represent people who otherwise would not have had access to lawyers otherwise. This generated even less money than my meager legal aid salary, and required almost 40,000 miles of driving per year to cases for clients referred by nonprofits all over the state. It was unbelievably rewarding, but going to so many courthouses meant new judges having new opportunities for the same old transphobic tricks: demanding genital inspections, deadnaming me, smirking when they did so. I passed well enough for cis, but having my deadname still on the ARDC website meant that anyone who ran an internet search on my name would learn I was trans almost immediately. Given that almost every opposing attorney did just that and then filed some kind of brief complaining about it, rare was the case where my gender identity *didn't* become an issue.

Worst of all, getting another job was out of the question *because* I'm trans. I applied to a position at a civil rights firm, only to be told that though I was the best candidate, "You would make our clients uncomfortable." Other legal aid clinics I applied to told me they didn't want to be seen as "taking a side" on the "trans issue." In short, if I wanted to practice law in Illinois as a trans person, I was on my own.

So I lit my career on fire and sued the Illinois Attorney Registration and Disciplinary Commission for allowing attorneys and judges to be transphobic unchecked.

MY PLAN WAS SIMPLE: to ask the ARDC to ratify *Bostock v. Clayton County*, the 2020 U.S. Supreme Court case in which Justice Gorsuch, writing for the majority, had held that "it is impossible to discriminate against a person for being homosexual or transgender without discriminating against that individual based on sex." Since the Illinois Rules of Professional Conduct – the ethics rules governing attorneys – already prohibited discrimination by attorneys on the basis of sex, I argued that *Bostock*'s reasoning should apply, and sought a declaratory judgment stating that the ethics rules *also* banned discrimination on the basis of gender identity or sexual orientation. In short, I was seeking a court order that the ethics rules prohibited the kind of transphobia I had been experiencing.

But I also knew that I had picked a fight I knew I couldn't win on the merits. As a branch of the Illinois state government – the ARDC is an organ of the Illinois Supreme Court – the agency has sovereign immunity, which means it cannot be sued without its consent. Rather unsurprisingly, the ARDC was not about to grant that consent willingly. Further, the ARDC had plenary power to discipline attorneys, which meant I was essentially hanging a giant bullseye on my law license. It was only a matter of time before I would be punished for what was, in truth, a move that was either incredibly audacious or remarkably stupid.

I also had to represent myself. The danger of this was also not lost on me; the saying in the law that a person who represents themselves has a fool for a client is generally a truism. Ordinarily, a lawyer representing themselves lacks the objectivity necessary to competently prosecute or defend the matter. But even if I could have afforded another lawyer for this on the little money I received from my "pay what you can" practice, I couldn't find a lawyer even willing to take the case. Most attorneys told me the profession simply wasn't ready for a transgender lawyer and to leave well enough alone. Several others weren't willing to suffer the harm that would inevitably come to their careers by suing the ARDC, even though they sympathized with my cause.

But truthfully I didn't expect to win. Instead, my hope was to bring attention to the fight, to show how trans people in Illinois courts were treated. In a best case scenario, maybe I could change the rules. And to show that was my goal, I offered the ARDC a deal. If they ratified *Bostock*, if they acknowledged gender identity was a protected ground from discrimination, I would pay their court costs. In short, I offered to pay the ARDC money to do the right thing. Given that Mercedes and I were paycheck to paycheck, I had to start saving money to do it.

But the ARDC wasn't interested in settling. Instead, for months, as the legal battle waged on, the agency took the hard-line position that they had plenary power to exclude anyone they wanted from the practice of law or from antidiscrimination rules, for any reason. In short, the ARDC wrote in legal filings that if they wanted to only allow cis white straight men to practice law, they had the authority to do so. As such, they argued that I had no legal right to challenge their power.

The fight went to three different courts in Illinois – the circuit court of Cook County, the Appellate Court, and the Supreme Court of Illinois. After both the Circuit Court and Supreme Court declined to hear the case, deferring to the ARDC's authority, I sued the ARDC in the United States District Court for the Northern District of Illinois, arguing that the ARDC's refusal to protect trans people violated the right to equal protection of the laws in the Fourteenth Amendment of the United States Constitution. This brought the Illinois Attorney General into the case, and their office misgendered me in much of the correspondence

between us – an added indignity, given the Democratic administration governing Illinois.

The litigation lasted for over a year. I was misgendered
multiple times by attorneys who publicly called themselves
allies as part of an elected Democratic administration. The
ARDC posted to my public attorney records on their website that
I was being investigated and disciplined for attorney misconduct, even though I had committed no misconduct and they'd
never notified me of any investigation. Later they termed that
public statement as an inadvertent error accidentally generated
by their system. Every week, I reiterated my offer to dismiss the
case and pay the ARDC's court costs if they would simply stipu-
late that the Illinois Rules of Professional Conduct prohibited
anti-trans discrimination. And every week, the ARDC's attorneys would reject that proposal and restate their position that
they could exclude anyone from the practice of law they wanted,
for any reason.

But what was most gratifying about the litigation was the
number of phone calls and emails I received from other trans
lawyers in Illinois.

When I had first called the ARDC years earlier, I had been
told I was the only trans lawyer in the state. That wasn't true, of
course; in a state with twelve and a half million people and over
62,000 lawyers, there was just no way that I was the only
attorney who happened to be transgender. What *was* true was
that there were very few who were *openly* trans, because of the
sheer degree of systemic discrimination that existed in the Illinois courts. It seemed as though every day I was talking with a
different lawyer whose career existed under a name and gender
identity that were lies, adopted to conform to the cisheteronormative expectations of a conservative field and judiciary. And
every one told me the same thing: They wanted to be out, *needed*
to be out, but couldn't be, because they were terrified they'd lose
their license, be sexually harassed or assaulted, or break down
upon being publicly misgendered or deadnamed. Before long, I

was getting calls and emails from trans lawyers in other states too, who saw the same conditions in their own jurisdictions.

The groundswell of support led to organizations like the National Lawyers Guild and Equality Illinois giving public statements of support, for which I am eternally grateful. Faced with institutional pressure, the ARDC finally caved. And on April 14, 2022, the ARDC stipulated that *Bostock* applied to the Illinois Rules of Professional Conduct. A month later, the Rules were formally amended to officially ban gender identity discrimination. A year after that, the Rules were amended again, this time incorporating the Illinois Human Rights Act, and banning any attorney from discriminating on the basis of a protected class. Now, for the first time, anyone really could be an attorney in Illinois.

"We won," I posted on Twitter later that day. I was literally in tears. Trans kids could grow up to be lawyers.

IN SOME WAYS, the victory was surreal. I certainly hadn't expected it. If I'm being honest, I had expected to fight to the end, lose, maybe even lose my license for trying. Most people who found out about the case told me I was either very brave or very foolish – or both.

But truthfully, it wasn't bravery. Bravery requires fear, because without fear, there is nothing through which to persevere. I wasn't afraid of the ARDC. I was afraid of what not having this fight would make me.

The biggest mistakes of my life had been fights I was unwilling to have. I walked away from fighting my parents for custody of my youngest sister. I didn't challenge my mother on her prejudice and bigotry until after I was out of her house. I wasn't going to make that mistake again. Certainly I was anxious – I am anxious before every court hearing, for every client. A client's freedom or livelihood or home is at stake, and being anxious, being nervous, shows that I care. The day I stop being nervous before a hearing is the day I stop being a lawyer.

But in a strange way, once you've been waterboarded, subjected to conversion therapy, told you should never have been born, had a knife held to your throat...you know how to survive.

EIGHTEEN

There is a tendency in the media to view transness as something to be avoided. We are depicted in terms of what transness causes – suicidality, depression, discrimination. Parents worry about trans people ruining their children's innocence, seeing transness as an outcome they don't want for their children. Even our allies often focus on the pain we endure at the hands of systemic and institutional discrimination. And certainly, my story has a good deal of that. The first two decades of my life certainly epitomized that.

But that's not the whole story. And pretending otherwise wouldn't just be a disservice to you, to the trans community, and to myself, it would also be a lie. I didn't survive everything in the preceding pages just for its own sake. I survived from the belief that at the other side, there would be a better future. There would be laughter.

There would be joy. Transness is a celebration of life, the refusal to allow the vagaries of societal backwardness to contain the human spirit. If there is pain in the trans experience, it is not intrinsic to transness, but rather external from it, the result of people unwilling to countenance the free expression of humanity disconnected from predetermined gender roles. Transness is joy because transness is, at its core, the belief that everything is possible, that boundaries exist to be broken, and that your journey is limited only by your imagination.

Transness is a paean to the human experience. And my story is no exception.

After the legal aid clinic closed, I landed a job offer with a large nonprofit that offered benefits and a hefty salary. But Mercedes, who I'd only been dating a few months yet already knew me better than anyone ever had, saw my hesitation.

"I don't think representing wealthy old white people is where your heart is," she said. "And your heart is what I want."

And then, to my utter shock, Mercy told me to find a way to represent marginalized people, people of color, and trans people, finances be damned. And with her encouragement and blessing, I opened a sliding scale law practice for people who could otherwise not afford lawyers, focusing on defending people in eviction, foreclosure, and criminal cases. It seemed somehow appropriate given my own journey. The work is hard. A "pay what you can" practice model isn't conducive to profitability and money is always tight, and driving all over a state larger than many European countries means putting in excess of 40,000 miles on my car every year. That's in addition to the stress of the cases themselves, which often involve people facing homelessness or incarceration. But it's incredibly rewarding, and it's an opportunity to leave the world a better place than I found it.

Mercedes and I got married on October 1, 2022, at the EAA aviation museum in Wisconsin. Appropriately enough, our ceremony took place before an array of World War II allied fighters in what she and I jokingly called "the ultimate antifa wedding." Sahreen, of course, was a bridesmaid, and Matt walked me down the aisle. It's difficult to describe just how beautiful Mercedes was that day, but one of my bridesmaids, my dear friend Jill, warned me that I would cry tears of joy when I saw her. She wasn't wrong. It was – and remains — the happiest day of my life.

What drew me to Mercy initially was her beauty, but what made me fall in love with her was her spirit. Mercy, like me, is trans, but unlike me she has a fearlessness that I simply adore. Early on, I learned that she had a simple rule of making sure she would be seen in any space trans people are unwelcome. She's a storyteller, an artist with words of a talent I doubt I'll ever see again, and I admire that about her. But what I have learned from her in three years of marriage is rather different: what love looks like. Never once has she raised her voice or a hand to me. But I do fall asleep in her arms every night with a smile on my lips.

When I was eight years old and dancing in the forest of my dreams, I longed for a life like the one I have now. When I was a teenager, I despaired, believing that a life like this would forever be beyond my reach. Now, I am living it. I am the culmination of my younger self's wildest dreams. And yet what is so remarkable about that fact is how mundane those dreams really were.

I have a glorious life. I get to awaken every morning to the sound of my beloved's heartbeat and the song of our two conures, Kathryn Janeway and Tuvok. If you passed me walking with Mercy on the street and did not know us, you would think of us as two women in love, for that is, at bottom, what we are. Maybe you see us at our weekly lunch with Sahreen and Gene, or at the movies, or at a Chicago Dogs or Schaumburg Boomers baseball game. *We are normal.* It is, in truth, all anyone ever wants.

In Jewish numerology, eighteen is a number of no small significance. It is the value of the Hebrew word *chai*, meaning life. My life is a celebration – and that is why I ended this book with the eighteenth chapter.

EPILOGUE

In 2024, on my 36th birthday of all days, I became the first openly trans attorney to orally argue at the Seventh Circuit Court of Appeals. It wasn't something I planned ahead of time. The case – representing a Palestinian tenant *pro bono* who was being evicted for displaying a Palestinian flag in her window – was a righteous cause near and dear to me personally. In the weeks leading up to the argument, with practice sessions interspersed with my regular court schedule, it honestly didn't even occur to me whether a trans attorney had previously argued there. Then, on the way home with Mercedes – whose birthday present to me was taking off work to see her wife argue at a federal court of appeals for the first time – I asked her whether she thought other trans attorneys arguing there had been as nervous as I had been.

"Have there even been other trans attorneys?" I asked.

The next day, I called the office of the Clerk of the Seventh Circuit and asked just that. To their knowledge, no other openly trans attorney had argued orally before the Court. That suspicion was confirmed a couple of weeks later by the results of a docket search.

It was a strange feeling. Even a case that had nothing to do with me was impacted by my gender identity. The little girl who at six years old just wanted to dance in the woods with long hair and ribbons never in her wildest dreams would have imagined being any kind of trailblazer. I certainly never set out to be.

As I've been writing this book, I've recalled a conversation I'd had with Matt a couple of years ago, at my wedding to Mercedes.

"If you had to change anything, would you?" he asked me. "Would you change how your parents treated you, the abuse from Ashley?"

I thought for a moment, considering. My answer, when it came, surprised both of us in its vehemence.

"Absolutely not."

In no way is this to excuse what my parents did, or what *I* did. I certainly would not advocate for my parents' peculiar brand of ostensible parenting to be replicated. But in a strange way, I owe my parents a debt of gratitude. I would not have become the woman I am today if not for them. There are still times I mourn for the life I never had, the girlhood I was denied, the experiences I will never know. I will never get to wear a slinky dress and get kissed at prom or know the angst of high school. I will never have any kind of mother-daughter bonding. I couldn't be my father's little girl, or dance with him at my wedding. In their place are memories of fear, of horror, of sadness.

Moreover, even beyond the truism that no person is ever solely responsible for their own successes, I am also cognizant of how much my life, my accomplishments, are because of luck or otherwise ill-begotten: a lucky test day on the SAT. Being born to an upper middle class white family. My father's connections at NBC. My listing of my race as "other" on applications to college and law school. Where I am now, *who* I am now, is a debt I owe to other people, and it is a debt I want *and need* to repay.

With all of this, you may be wondering *why* I wouldn't want to do anything differently. The answer is simple. But what I received through those memories is an understanding that we are more than the worst moments of our lives and the worst decisions we ever make. Those are a part of me, yes, but they need not define me. It is for that reason I won't say I would do things differently: To say that would be to dismiss who I am now, who I have become, as the fruit of a poisonous tree. I cannot accept that.

But at the same time, I can accept the duality of lessons my life offers. To all outward appearances, my family was normal. The county reviewers who came by every six months never had any reason to suspect that my parents – my father, the respectable man with a doctorate who worked as an audio engineer and had covered presidents on Air Force One; my mother, the beautiful young woman who had dabbled in acting and modeling – were anything else. Nor did my parents make any attempt to hide their bigotries, openly complaining to the county reviewer about "Spanish" people and "Negroes" taking their jobs and how "negroes can't decide what they want to be called." My parents were normal because their prejudice was normal, even in a blue, Democratic state like Maryland. My parents were normal because their prejudice was merely "politics."

But political disagreements cause harm. My parents' "politics" were racism, homophobia, and transphobia. What Republicans mean when they say parents should be allowed to raise their children as they see fit, free of government interference, is that parents like mine should be given carte blanche to torture their trans and queer children into living in denial. I am living proof that what that method creates is not straight or cis people, but rather undead husks, harming other people and themselves out of sheer apathy. It is a road to intergenerational trauma, not any kind of morality.

Trans children exist. I know because I was one. I grew up, and became a trans adult. And I did so because transness is inherent, transness is immutable, and most of all, transness is something that cannot – and should not – be undone.

NOTES

INTRODUCTION

i. Blue Telusma, *Before You Share 'Trauma Porn' Videos on Social Media Consider These Critical Things*, The Grio (Apr. 4, 2019), https://thegrio.com/2019/04/04/nipsey-hussle-trauma-porn-social-media-blue-telusma/.

ii. Nagle, R. (2024) *By the Fire We Carry: The Generations-Long Fight for Justice on Native Land*. S.I.: HarperCollins.

FIVE

i. *Conversion Therapy* (2018) American Academy of Child and Adolescent Psychiatry. Available at: https://www.aacap.org/aacap/Policy_Statements/2018/Conversion_Therapy.aspx (Accessed: 26 January 2025).

ii. *Conversion Therapy* (no date) *Merriam-Webster Dictionary*. Available at: https://www.merriam-webster.com/dictionary/conversion%20therapy (Accessed: 26 January 2025).

iii. Ryan C, Toomey RB, Diaz RM, Russell ST. Parent-Initiated Sexual Orientation Change Efforts With LGBT Adolescents: Implications for Young Adult Mental Health and Adjustment. J Homosex. 2020;67(2):159-173. doi: 10.1080/00918369.2018.1538407. Epub 2018 Nov 7. PMID: 30403564; PMCID: PMC10371222.

FOURTEEN

i. Nalick, Anna. "Breathe (2 AM)." *Breathe*. Columbia, 2004.

ACKNOWLEDGMENTS

This is my second book (a sentence I admittedly never expected to write a decade ago), and both have shown just how true it is that no one ever does anything of note alone. Indeed, every true accomplishment is a collective effort, and this is no exception.

First and foremost, I owe a great debt – and my heart – to my beautiful wife Mercedes, the love of my life, my best friend, and the best thing that's ever happened to me. Through her love, all things are possible.

Thank you especially to my chosen sister Sahreen, who believes in me even when I don't believe in myself. I've written two books now, and they were both your ideas; these are as much your books as they are mine. You are one of the finest people I have ever had the privilege of knowing. I cannot thank you enough for being the amazing person you are, and I love you so much.

My dear friend MaTt Koplow, my oldest friend, who is mentioned multiple times in these pages; thank you for fighting for me when I was not yet able to fight for myself. I would not be alive if it wasn't for you. Adrienne, my dear friend and maid of honor; I appreciate you more than you know. Kliff Svatos – you gave me a map when I was lost, and you did it with love, and if not for you I wouldn't be here. You are such a blessing in my life. Jill Manrique, you are a badass and everything I want to be in life, and I hope you know how lucky everyone is who knows you.

I am eternally grateful to the acceptance and love I received from Mercy's family – her parents (my in-laws) Donna and John, her brother (my brother in law) Roe'don, and her (and now my) niece and nephews.

I owe gratitude to my parents, because without them my story would not exist. I hope through reading this you can finally understand your eldest daughter. And to my sisters – Sabrina, I have always admired your grace, your tenacity, and your ability to add to the sum total of the universe with your music. Elaina, if you had written this book, with your gifted pen and equally gifted wit, it would be both better and funnier. To both of you, I wish things had been different between us. To my grandparents, of blessed memory, this book is for you; I may not have carried on the family name, but I hope I nonetheless added something positive to its legacy.

For my dear friend Patrick Stinson, one of my oldest friends, thank you for giving me a chance those many years ago and showing what true friendship actually is. My mentors, Lesley Williams and Kelly Kleiman, are the very best of us and examples of the woman I want to be. Shana Bartels, a dear friend, officiated at my wedding to Mercy and I owe her forever for doing so. My life has gifted me too many dear friends to list here, but suffice to say I am forever grateful to the many people who have made my story possible. If a life is the sum total of one's experiences, then it is also the sum total of one's relationships, and thus I am a very lucky woman indeed.

To Dr. Herb Smith, you didn't realize it at the time, but you showed me a light at the end of a very dark tunnel, and I will always be indebted to you for that. To Dr. Susan Scott, you gave me joy in the darkest time of my life, and thus I will forever be grateful to you, Aunt Sue.

This book would literally not exist without the invaluable assistance and contributions of so many people, including Lorelei O'Hagan, Terijian, and Ray, among many others, who spent their scarcest resource – their time – making this better. I cannot thank them enough.

Thank you to lawyers like Christina DiEdoardo, Gerard O'Toole, Eliza Orlins, Kristen Zornada, Kimber Russell, and Madiba Dennie, and to every public defender and legal aid lawyer in the United States. You epitomize the best part of this profession and it's an honor and privilege to call so many of you my friends.

Thank you also to the people who taught me what solidarity and a life worth living actually mean — in no particular order, Emma Goldman, Angela Davis, Ta-Nehisi Coates, Barbara Smith, Audre Lorde, bell hooks, Brene Brown, Mariame Kaba, Kelly Hayes, Judith Butler, Paule Marshall, Angela Butler, Ursula K. LeGuin, Langston Hughes, Maya Angelou, Paule Marshall, Gregory Maguire, Rabbi Danya Ruttenberg, John Brown, Thaddeus Stevens, Eliza Orlins, Clarence Darrow, Ilhan Omar, Cori Bush, Rashida Tlaib, Lexi Alexander, Alexandra Halaby, Feminista Jones (Dr. Michelle Taylor), Judith Butler, and Julia Serrano — for writing brilliant and beautiful words that led me on the path to one day, G-d willing, becoming a person I can actually be proud of. Though I never had the privilege of meeting these great people, I nonetheless hope I have proven a worthy student of their examples.

Any errors in this book are mine alone.

Free Palestine, from the river to the sea.